THE Skeleton at the Plough,

OR THE POOR FARM LABOURERS OF THE WEST;

WITH THE
AUTOBIOGRAPHY AND REMINISCENCES
OF
GEORGE MITCHELL,
"ONE FROM THE PLOUGH,"

EDITED BY
STEPHEN PRICE.

LONDON:
GEORGE POTTER, Beehive Office, 10, Bolt Court, Fleet Street,
and 5, Catherine Street, Strand.
T. ROBERTS & Co., Red Lion Court, Fleet Street.

LEAMINGTON:
J. E. M. VINCENT, Labourer's Union Chronicle Office.

Printed by H. & W. Brown, 261, Brompton Road, London.

THE SKELETON AT THE PLOUGH.

OR THE

Poor Farm Labourers of the West,

WITH THE

AUTOBIOGRAPHY AND REMINISCENCES

OF

GEORGE MITCHELL,

"ONE FROM THE PLOUGH."

Edited by

STEPHEN PRICE.

LONDON:

G. POTTER, Beehive Office, 10, Bolt Court, Fleet Street,
And 5, Catherine Street, Strand.

CONTENTS.

Introduction. PAGE

CHAP. I. The Early English Style somewhat decorated. 1

CHAP. II. The half-way house on the labourer's road to ruin. 7

CHAP. III. The good old times about the beginning of the nineteenth century. 10

CHAP. IV. On steam locomotion and reform, with a little political gossip. 15

CHAP. V. One-sided Free Trade, an enemy to the working classes. 19

CHAP. VI. Foreign manufactures and British industry. 23

CHAP. VII. John Bull, licensed dealer in beer, cider, wine, spirits and tobacco—to be drunk on the premises. 29

CHAP. VIII. A few more words about beer, cider, wine, spirits and tobacco. 33

CHAP. IX. Gold discovery, a friend to the rich and an enemy to the poor. 40

CHAP. X. The condition of the poor farm labourers of the West before the dawn of Union. 44

CHAP. XI. The romantic cottages of the West and the rural felicity enjoyed by our friends in their " homes." 52

CHAP. XII. The educational status of the farm labourers, how they live, and the enlightenment of our rural parishes. 61

CHAP. XIII. An ecclesiastical phenomenon in the Church of England—a clergyman who raised his voice in the cause of the oppressed. 77

		PAGE.
CHAP. XIV.	The great Arch of the union bridge that will carry the men safe over.	84
CHAP. XV.	Rules and constitution of the National Agricultural Labourers Union.	89
CHAP. XVI.	Autobiography and recollections of "One from the plough."	95
CHAP. XVII.	A glance at my native village, and how I came to leave it.	102
CHAP. XVIII.	A pilgrimage from poverty to competence	109
CHAP. XIX.	Autobiography concluded. How I came to take up the cause of the agricultural labourers.	116
CHAP. XX.	A meeting at my native village and the formation of a branch.	122
CHAP. XXI.	The first annual Whitsuntide meeting of farm labourers, on Ham Hill, 1873.	128
CHAP. XXII.	Prejudice, persecution and prosecution.	143
CHAP. XXIII.	Where are we now?	147
CHAP. XXIV.	Conclusion. The cause and the cure.	154

ERRATA.

Page 15—7th line for "Robert" read, George.

Note to page 46—1th line for "increasing" read, unceasing.

INTRODUCTION.

IN October, 1874, the West of England was greatly startled and shocked by the little engraving which appears on the cover of this book, orignally drawn as an embellishment to a handbill announcing Labourers' Meetings in Somerset and Dorsetshire.

Noblemen and members of parliament, with a host of parsons, magistrates and country gentry, denounced the sketch as a gross exaggeration of the state of the Farm Labourers, and as calculated to produce discontent in the minds of the peasantry, who were represented as hitherto living in sylvan happiness and peace, greatly attached to their employers, and looking up to the landowners as parental beings, from whose hospitable mansions were dispensed blankets, coals, soup, port wine, brandy, baby-linen and every other blessing that this world could afford.

At the Agricultural Dinners, Ploughing Matches, Labourer's Friend (?) Societies, and other gatherings of landlords and tenants, mention was made of the "skeleton at the plough," and it would have been almost as safe to have offered a reward of £10,000 to any after dinner speaker on these occasions who did not denounce Mr. Mitchell's "Skeleton" as to those who had not animadverted upon "agitators who go about setting class against class."

And what reason was there for putting forth such a hideous caricature of the farm labourer? Though it is admitted on all hands that he is half starved, and though it is looked upon by some as the wise but mysterious will of the Almighty that it should be so, he is after all, not in literal reality an unclothed skeleton, or as some old-fashioned Somersetshire folks would say "a notamy."

Why, therefore, should he be represented as a figure of death? Why should he be sketched as a walking ghost?

The answer to these very natural queries which, in fact, have been frequently put to us by friend and foe, will be found in this volume which we offer to the reading public, chiefly as a collection of facts illustrating the history of the Agricultural Labourers' movement in the West of England, and the part we have taken therein.

An old adage says "There is a skeleton in every house," and as "The Skeleton in the Cupboard," "The Skeleton at the Old Barn," 'at the Parsonage,' 'at the Manor-house,' and at various other places,—were, at one time, favourite titles for books, we shall make no apology for our title of "THE SKELETON AT THE PLOUGH."

THE SKELETON AT THE PLOUGH.

CHAPTER I.

THE EARLY ENGLISH STYLE, SOMEWHAT DECORATED.

WE don't propose going back further than Adam who is alleged to have been first a horticulturist and then an agricultural labourer, and who, with that fatherless girl Eve formed the first union ever heard of, nor will we say much about these poor but dishonest parents of ours who lost a very good place through apple-stealing, since being orphans with neither father nor mother to tell them better, we can make every excuse for them; nor shall we describe the scriptural farm labourer who is so much spoken of in the Bible, anent which our hyper-professing readers if we have any, would do well to delve a little into The Book and get themselves up in divine equity on the land and labour question:—Even

Agricola and Cincinnatus will not be more than named here, the agricolæ of Cincinnati would receive more notice at our hands had we time and space to devote to the world at large:—we have enough to do to lay before our "kyind" friends the state of our farm labourers past and present, and possibly to vaticinate slightly as to their future, though prophecy after the fact is much the safer of the two. And as we do not belong to any Archæological Society, though why not, we know not, we shall not attempt any pictures of the Ancient British or Anglo-Saxon ploughman, but will skim lightly the surface of history, staying to notice only one or two things very patent and apparent to all who dip for the truth, while they skim over the lore of the past.

We suspect that the Agricultural Labourer was not badly off at the Norman Conquest. He had been subjected to some amount of turmoil and change under the alternate rules of Saxon and Dane, but though we are accustomed to plume ourselves upon the stability of our present institutions and pray "Give peace in our time, O Lord!" it is probable that unsettled times were less disastrous to those who lived by the sweat of their brow, than to their wealthier countrymen who so often had to "stand and deliver" the gains of a few peaceful years to the greed and rapacity of a victorious faction. The reigns of Alfred and Canute were more advantageous to the "laboured hind" than those of the Williams and Georges of later times, for it is certain that the little people held land, and whensoever, wheresoever, and under whomsoever this was the case, they were happier and more prosperous than is the land-moiler of these piping times of peace under the boasted reign of Queen Victoria.

Be that as it may, the Norman Conquest introduced an entirely new element into the country. No sooner had the Saxon king, Harold, succumbed to the Norman arrow, than almost the whole of the country became, like the "fair land of Poland" of Balfe *note*riety, "ploughed by the hoof" of Norman barons and knights;—brigands, filibusters, freebooters in fact, whose sole idea of reward for their zealous and sanguinary following of William the Norman, was a foothold upon the fertile lands of England.

They were a poor, ignorant, superstitious and brutal lot of fellows, were these Norman nobility, so cowardly that they cased themselves in steel and brass from top to toe, and even dared not show their faces but closed up their countenances with iron shutters while their followers were half naked or clothed only in leather jerkins. Armorial bearings, of which the so-called "County Families"* of this kingdom are so proud, originated in the ignorant and unlettered condition of the knights and barons who could neither read nor write, and as they could not see each others faces when the shutters were up, they were obliged to have door-plates on their armour.† If they had ever learnt their ABC, and how to spell out a name,

---

* One would have thought that all families in a county were county families, but there are certain people who have had the privilege of slicing up the counties among themselves and of setting all the other people in the county to work for them, mostly at starvation wages, in order that they, the privileged ones, might live in indolence and be worshipped by the toilers as "County-Families."

† We are indebted to the Rev. Mr. White's delightful little work "Landmarks of the History of England" for this idea.

these plates would doubtless have been inscribed thus :—

| Sir Iohn Smith, Kt. | or | BARON JONES. |

but as such inscriptions would have signified nothing to men who had not learnt their letters, a little picture was substituted forming a kind of hieroglyphic, while the mottoes were doubtless added by monks who lived by begging and humbly placed what little learning they possessed at the service of this Christian chivalry, who kindly patronised their religion as a sort of thing that was necessary to keep the conquered race subservient and contented, by giving them hopes beyond the skies, in exchange for earthly prospects which had been ruthlessly taken from them.

We must not, however, be too hard upon the monks of old. They were the only guardians of the poor and the only poor-rate collectors; they built all the cathedrals, abbeys, and parish churches; they founded the great universities; maintained hospitals, gratuitous hotels, schools and asylums of various kinds. Thus, they did more with the offerings of the people than the "Reformed" Church has ever done with all her vast accumulations of stolen property.

Nor can we accuse William the Conqueror of stealing the people's lands. He merely set his nobles, knights and squires over the people as stewards, never dreaming of anything so unjust as to deprive the common folk of their right to cultivate a portion of the land upon which they were born, much less to deny them dwelling-room. The rude monarch never supposed but that the land was as much at the service of the people as the atmosphere or the sea. Austere as he was, he had not enough of the refinement of cruelty in his composition to think of divorcing God's creatures from God's earth. It was left for the descendants of the king's creatures to perpetrate this monstrous, vile, and crying iniquity!

But we were saying that a new element was introduced at the Conquest. The country was overrun by a set of proud, stuck-up, ignorant people, without an idea in their heads save that of family pride, punctilio, and conscious self-importance. They have sat like incubi upon Old England for more than eight hundred years and they have never changed and never will; like the Bourbons, they forget nothing, learn nothing. No matter what attempts at progress the people make, these old men of the sea are ever re-actionary and do somehow succeed in keeping the millions from exercising their will. They must have a serpent-like fascination about them, and the people who are fascinated must be very much of the rabbit tribe to be thus attracted in order to be swallowed! but more of this further on. We now conclude our first chapter by pointing out that the new element of chivalry and aristocracy introduced at the Norman Conquest was an injury to the peasantry of this country because it made equality impossible, and whatever militates against equality, lowers the lower class, whereas, if equality were possible of attainment, it must be self-evident that a lower class would cease to exist, for all the people composing it would be elevated to equal rank with those who are now termed the "upper and middle class," and this might yet be accomplished. Perchance the School Board may do it, nay, it most certainly would, if education were free, secular, and compulsory to the letter, and all the schools were brought under government control, but the Norman element has prevented this, and only part of our dream of equality will come to pass in this country for very many years to come, but we venture to hope that in our life-time, more will be done to throw off the yoke of the conqueror's followers than has been accomplished in eight hundred years. The late Mr. Percy B. Shelley addresses our Agricultural labourers and working classes in general as follows :—

> Men of England, wherefore plough
> For the lords who lay ye low?
> Wherefore weave with toil and care,
> The rich robes your tyrants wear?
>
> Wherefore feed, and clothe, and save,
> From the cradle to the grave,
> Those ungrateful drones who would
> Drain your sweat—nay, drink your blood!
>
> Wherefore, Bees of England, forge
> Many a weapon, chain, and scourge,
> That these stingless drones may spoil
> The forced produce of your toil?
>
> Have ye leisure, comfort, calm,
> Shelter, food, love's gentle balm?
> Or what is it ye buy so dear
> With your pain and with your fear?
>
> The seed ye sow, another reaps;
> The wealth ye find another keeps;
> The robes ye weave, another wears;
> The arms ye forge, another bears!
>
> Shrink to your cellars, holes, and cells;
> In halls ye deck, another dwells.
> Why shake the chains ye wrought? Ye see
> The steel ye tempered glance on ye.

> With plough, and spade, and hoe, and loom,
> Trace your grave, and build your tomb,
> And weave your winding-sheet, till fair
> England be your sepulchre!
>
> Nay, sow—but let no tyrant reap;
> Find wealth—let no impostor heap;
> Weave robes,—let not the idle wear;
> Forge arms,—in your defence to bear!

We, however, don't quite agree with Mr. Shelley although his sentiments are worth consideration. At present we advise ploughmen and all other toilers to work for anybody who will pay a fair day's wages for a fair day's work.

CHAPTER II.

The Half-way House on the Labourer's Road to Ruin.

THE "Glorious Revolution" of 1688 though not a half-way house on the high road of time from where we started, may be considered as an intermediate station on the road to ruin, a road which the poor farm-labourers of the West have been travelling for centuries past. Drayton, the river poet of that time describes the happy condition of our peasantry, and a critic of to-day writing of the comparative state of our streams and our people then and now says:—"Surely in these matters the world has changed sadly for the worse. In Drayton's day there was merriment enough among the country folk, when the mirthful clowns danced with their lasses to the music of pipe and tabor on the village green. It might be hazardous to affirm that just as surely as our rivers were once dainty, silvery, full, and fair—just as surely as they are now black, poisonous, filthy, shameful—so our hinds were once really joyous; and, in spite of civil wars and turmoils, England was merry."

It is certain therefore that there was no Skeleton at the Plough in those days. The people *could* be merry then, because they had enough food.

He further remarks:—" When the Thames was sweet, and salmon was common fare, there was a charming, but now lost, form of culture in England. The life that clowns and ploughmen led ' when Tom came home from labour and Cis from milking Rose,' was sweetened by dance and song, and cheered with stories, glad or pitiful. There was a native peasant art in all these things, just as there was a traditional costume. The pleasures of the existence of the southern fisherman or shepherd in Sicily or in Greece were common here. We know this for certain, because we find, from scraps of old ballad, that English peasants sang songs which are still to be heard at the village dances in Greece and in Italy. The strife and pressure of modern times has crushed out all this peasant-culture, and we can no more replace it than we can make the Avon recall back the waves that floated past under the eyes of SHAKESPEARE," and he wisely concludes that " We can only determine that knowledge shall increase with all its light and all its temporary dangers. The task to be undertaken for the rivers, and for the peasantry who dwell on their banks, is at bottom the same—the restoration of the benefits that modern life has taken away."

But now, why do we select the advent of William of Orange as a half-way house on the road to ruin? Why, because during the short and retrogressive reign of his predecessor, James the Second, was perpetrated the shameful deprivation of all the labourer's rights in the land, which he held as surely as the knight or the squire.

Lord Carnarvon said, in a late speech at Newbury, that an act had been passsed under an earlier reign which entitled every tiller of the soil to four acres of land attached to his cottage, and his lordship regarded this act as "groping in the dark" and quite approved of its repeal, but we would ask Lord Carnarvon has there been any groping in the *light* on the part of our legislature for an improvement in the condition of the Agricultural Labourer? Has not the whole history of our legislation upon the land been one long series of spoliations of the little men in the interests of the great ones? Has not the original agriculturist been dis-established and disendowed? Was not Naboth's vineyard confiscated by the Ahabs and Jezebels of the constitutional (?) and protestant times of William the Dutchman, and Anne, and the Georges? Are not our common lands filched by lords of the manor all over the country now? Lord Carnarvon once sent for us to confer upon the requirements of the Agricultural Labourers. We did'nt get much "change" out of each other because our aims and interests were incompatible. We are bent upon raising our old friends the Poor Farm Labourers of the West, while his lordship is equally determined to conserve the profits and emoluments of his class even at the risk of exterminating the men who have delved all their treasures out of the soil. If, however, Lord Carnarvon wants to know our opinion of the duty our legislators owe to the farm labourers, we unhesitatingly reply " Restore to the Farm Labourer the four acres of land—restore him his position as the last of the Stuarts found it when he came to the throne, or give him an equivalent out of your vastly increased rents, and let him have that voice in making the laws which the four acres of land would have entitled him to. *

CHAPTER III.

The Good Old Times about the beginning of the Nineteenth Century.

ALTHOUGH at the commencement of the present century the agricultural labourer had long ceased to be a land-holder and was sunk in ignorance, superstition and degradation of almost every kind, particularly in Hants, Wilts, Somerset, Dorset, and Devon, he, nevertheless, obtained enough to eat. In 1801 the combined wages and perquisites of the Western Farm Labourers amounted to 22s., reckoning the present purchasing power of his money,

---

* Not only was the Revolution an important station on the Labourer's Road to Ruin, but the Reformation had robbed the peasantry of their best friends, the Monks, who, with all their superstition, used church property, not to maintain genteel wives and expensive families, but to educate the young, cure the sick, and feed the poor.

and the present price of such provisions as were given him at that time; so that, though he was in a sadly dependent and servile condition, he was thrice as well off as he afterwards was before the formation of Labourers' Unions, and twice as well off as he now is in the West of England.

But these were days in which the "development" of the country was in its infancy, wherein no hissing, roaring, screaming machines of glittering steel and brass exceeding the elephant in weight and beating the race-horse for speed, invaded the quiet vales and rumbled under the hills of the rural districts; wherein no telegraph wires conveyed a subtle, soul-like fluid, containing the wishes and sentiments of men and women, from country to town, and from country to country: and, wherein, nought but wretched dame-schools imparted a knowledge of the alphabet to a favoured few of the children, while the sons of rich farmers and small gentry walked several miles a day to be mercilessly thrashed into the first simple rules of arithmetic and a few pages of the Eton Latin Grammar, by some red-nosed parson or pedagogue who knew very little himself but how to inflict the greatest amount of pain upon youths of tender years by the application of cane and birch.

This reminds us of a very good story about a head-master of Westminster School, who, one day, when the Bishop of London had dined with him, sent for two boys and gave each of them a terrible beating before the bishop. The Right Reverend Prelate naturally enquired what these boys had done to merit such a severe flogging, when the head-master replied "Oh, nothing, nothing my Lord!

But their father is an old friend of mine and he begged that I would take great pains with them. A good caning keeps the best of boys humble, and I thought that such a thrashing as that before the Bishop of London would give them something to remember and do them good for the whole of their lives." And then the learned doctors of divinity, conscious of having performed an important duty, stuck to their theology and port for the rest of the evening.

Living was much simpler among the gentry in those days than now. Had dinners *à la Russe* been introduced at that time, only kings, queens, dukes, and very rich earls would have thought of adopting them. The country gentleman dined at two o'clock on plain roast and boiled, only occasionally dining late on account of hunting or company. He did not as a rule drink wine at dinner, but he settled down to old port afterwards, and a bottle or two extra at a sitting did not signify much so long as he could depend upon the vintage. Precisely the same views as to quantity and quality were held by his spiritual adviser, who frequently dined and drank with the squire. He was generous and goodnatured on the whole to those who did not oppose him in any way, but he was an exacting tyrant who had been brought up to expect the homage of all about him. He compelled his servants to attend his church and his tenantry to vote as he did. And it is only fair to him to say that just as much homage as he exacted from his inferiors he religiously paid to his superiors. It was only for the neighbouring earl to say who was to be the next great man in politics or literature, and straightway the squire believed and obeyed and moulded the whole of public opinion in his district to the taste, the will, or caprice of his lordship.

In like manner, the countess, though perhaps the most ordinary of ladies, quite unconscious of her influence, entirely swayed the opinions of Madam Squire upon the merits of rival opera singers, the latest fashions, and altogether the tone that society should take with regard to religion, morals, and taste. Of course, the parson's wife, and the lawyer's wife, and the doctor's wife, retailed all this to other women, just as their husbands imbibed their politics from the squire, and hence the whole public opinion of the country was formed according to the wish and whim of the nobility.

But what we desire to show in this chapter, is, that the landlords themselves did not live in such luxury and grandeur in the year 1800 as they now do. They have increased four-fold, in some cases ten-fold in their wealth, and have improved wonderfully in their style of living, they have also somewhat gained in education and real civilization. There is, however, room for improvement still. More scientific and technical education is needed in our higher schools. Sons and heirs should travel more to complete their education and grow more cosmopolitan in their ideas, broader in their creeds, and more sensible in manner and conversation. But one thing is certain, the landlords are a far more luxurious class now than they were at the commencement of the present century.

Then the farmer,—how was it with him at the dawn of this era of braggadocio? (For it does not seem possible that any century could be so boastful of itself as this same nineteenth). Was he a well-educated gentleman of somewhat distinguished appearance, riding into the market town on his well-bred hunter, himself the equal of the lawyer, the parson, and the doctor? No, he was a coarse, dull, heavy kind of fellow, something between a cattle-drover and a prize-fighter, very ignorant, narrow-minded, and thick-headed. He lived in the plainest style, chiefly upon salt meat and any unsaleable farm produce, he sat down to his meals in his smockfrock or in his shirt sleeves, in hob-nailed boots and breeches reeking with manure. He regarded the squire's footman as his superior and called him "Sir." He was glad to obtain situations for his daughters in the household of his landlord, while his sons often enlisted in the army as an escape from the monotonous drudgery of farm labour to which they had early been condemned. His wife milked the cows, churned the butter and made the cheese. In short, the farmer was several grades lower in the social scale than he now is, and never dreamt of becoming the second heavy country gentleman he has done under the new regime.

The labourer was then almost the equal of the farmer, and it is well-known that the men lived as well as their masters, both obtaining a sufficiency of bacon and cabbage and both being therewith content.

CHAPTER IV.

ON STEAM LOCOMOTION AND REFORM, WITH A LITTLE POLITICAL GOSSIP.

WHEN the mail-coaches, vans and road waggons were replaced by locomotive engines, a revolution far more wonderful than that of a change of dynasties was effected in this country. And this revolution was brought about, not by any king, or general, or statesman, but by a far-seeing, ingenious, persevering working man. Robert Stevenson, although he prophesied great things for his new machine, was not prepared for the immense success that awaited him and the rapidity of the development of his idea that followed its first demonstration. Ten miles an hour was the modest aspiration of the North-Country Vulcan, but his first complete passenger engine* made thirty miles easily, and when the first train of local big-wigs ran up to London, they requested that the speed should be kept down to ten miles an hour, but Stevenson, who was on the engine, finding everything going on nicely and smoothly, put on the steam and forged ahead at the rate of half-a-mile a minute, so that

---

*This engine "The Rocket" together with two or three unsuccessful attempts, the "Sanspariel," "Puffing Billy," and other interesting relics of locomotive pioneering, are to be seen at the Patent Exhibition, South Kensington Museum.

the gentlemen discovered themselves in London some hours earlier than they expected. Well, this rapid rate of travelling caused a rapid rate of progress in every conceivable way, too rapid for the poor farm labourers as we shall presently show.

It is astonishing how soon we accommodate ourselves to altered circumstances. Even when the change is for the worse, men speedily forget those better times they have known, and cheerfully submit to privations of the most novel and perplexing kind. 'But when the alteration is for the better most persons accept the improvement, vast as it may be, with perfect equaniminity, and wonder how they ever got along at all under the old regime. So it was with the farmers, when railways invaded the far off rural districts. True, many of them had never visited London in their lives. The few exceptions had performed the journey under great difficulties, previously making their wills. They had travelled day and night on lumbering coach-tops, not without their fears of highwaymen, and liable in winter-time to have their progress either way checked by a snowstorm which might keep them prisoners at some wretched half-way house, the lawful prey of that lawyer-like being, so far as ingenuity in finding items for a long bill is concerned, namely, the hotel-keeper, who ruthlessly charged his victims day by day treble prices for bad rations, forced wine upon them they did not require, and saddled them with the cost of enough wax candles to light up the altar of a Roman Catholic cathedral. In addition to all this, coaching accidents, though not on such a large and horrifying scale as railway disasters, were much more frequent, and the loss of life was far greater, in proportion to the number of travellers, by coach than by rail.

Yet when the convenient train became the order of the day, the farmers took to railway travelling as ducks take to water; they often ran up to London to transact business, or to partake of the pleasures of the town, and they soon found that cattle, sheep and pigs, poultry, eggs, butter, milk and all other kinds of farm produce, would fetch double prices to what they had brought in the old days.

They were, however, not so surprised at their good luck as to double the wages of their poor relations the farm labourers, but quietly buttoned up their plethoric pockets with an inward chuckle, and told their wives not to let go any more eggs, milk, butter, cheese, bacon, pork, pig's fry or anything else to the men, as it could now be all sent to London and be turned into good money.

In the coaching days, the only means of forwarding produce to London was by road-waggon or canal-boat, both too slow to permit the conveyance of fresh provisions, besides which, the farmer didn't know the markets, and undervalued produce, so that if a labourer would take five shillings in money on a Saturday, he could have articles of food as well, worth to him now perhaps fifteen shillings, whereas, the railways so drain the provinces of these articles, that the poor man has to pay town prices out of village wages, and the result is semi-starvation.

Contemporaneously with the introduction of railway travelling, came some important changes of political opinion, leading up to the great Reform Bill of 1832, by which the electoral system was considerably altered, taking much of the political power out of the hands of the gentry, who were up to that time almost the sole electors of members of parliament, and giving it into the hands of the middle classes.

Now, although any extension of the suffrage is a boon, considered in the light of an instalment towards the full sum of political power due to the people of this country, namely, MANHOOD SUFFRAGE, (a goal which the working classes should strive as one man to reach), there can be no doubt but we grow the more conservative for a time, as we obtain these paltry dividends of the debt justly owing to us, for so soon as a new class is added to the happy number of the electoral elect, they evince a desire to keep out in the cold the other poor bloods who have not been included in the last reform. Hence, the people's sometime idol, Lord John Russell, though an earnest apostle of reform so far as his short-sighted glance could reach, became "Finality John" directly the word "household suffrage" was mentioned, and his utmost idea of liberality to the outsiders, was dropping a pound or two in the figure at which the renters should be enfranchised.

Nor did he evince a desire to re-distribute the seats with rigid impartiality, but left such wretched little constituencies as Andover, Chippenham, Devizes, Dorchester, Evesham, Horsham, Launceston, Lymington, Midhurst, Shaftesbury, Wareham, &c., of the still enfranchised little boroughs, and many others since happily disfranchised. Not that any town or district should be left without the privilege of exercising the right of voting, but equal electoral districts, including so many thousands of voters in each district, whether dwelling in cities, towns, villages or hamlets, should be established. This, with the abolition of canvassing and all hustings expenses, would make bribery and corruption well-nigh impossible.

The Reform Bill of 1832, although it was an important step towards the enfranchisement of the people, threw the direct responsibility of government chiefly into the hands of a class unconnected with the land, and as a consequence, measures were passed which accelerated the downward movement of the poor agricultural labourer.

CHAPTER V.

ONE-SIDED FREE TRADE, AN ENEMY TO THE WORKING CLASSES.

AN especial political feature, affecting the interests of the farm labourers during the first half of the nineteenth century, was the adoption of the principle of Free Trade in corn, under Sir Robert Peel. The landlords and farmers were desperately frightened about it and opposed the measure tooth and nail, fighting for every inch of the ground with true British valour and obstinacy. In 1844 an able pamphlet addressed to Mr. Disraeli was published, in which the writer anticipated great distress sooner or later among the agricultural labouring classes, arising from the free importation of wheat, and doubtless the loss occasioned by the remission of Foreign corn duties has fallen upon poor Hodge. The landlords have been raising their rents ever since. We know a farmer who has had nineteen notices to quit his farm in twenty-seven years, which has meant nothing more or less than nineteen rises in his rent! Yet, strange to say, the farmers have been doing better than ever, are better educated, live more elegantly and luxuriously, spend more money, and hold more than ever they did. But upon this point we would say to the landlords—

"'Lay not this flattering unction to your souls.'"
It is no more to your credit that you have usuriously increased the burdens of the farmers because they have been able by some other means to bear them. The burden has had to fall on some one. It *has* fallen upon the poor farm labourers of this country" Free-trade has caused an expansion in the incomes and the requirements of the upper and middle classes. It has created a vast demand for farm produce so that there is none of it to be spared for the producer. No, he got another shilling a week in lieu of five or six shillings worth of perquisites, and there he was, as we remember him, working for six or seven shillings a week with a very little thin beer or cider, mere acid to keep his galvanic apparatus going, in order that more work might be got out of him than his poor under-fed condition would otherwise permit; and just as the zinc in the telegraph boxes wears rapidly away as its force is daily and hourly extracted from it by the acid bath, so is the life and strength of the miserable land-drudge rapidly exhausted by the fermented sour-water acting upon

a stomach unlubricated by proper nourishment.

Free-trade has not benefitted any of the lower classes of this country. It has done them harm. It has secured them a cheap loaf, but it has compelled them to live too much on that one article of food. "Man shall not live by bread alone" saith the scriptures, and we desire to apply this fiat literally to the people of England, for very much of the grand politics of the Bible are rendered inoperative through the application of too much spiritual interpretation, by those, probably, who don't find it convenient to carry out the plain temporal meaning of the text. We therefore take the liberty of reversing this process for once and repeat "Man shall not live by bread alone." He must have beef and mutton. If anybody is to eat beef and mutton—aye venison, hare, partridge, pheasant, salmon, turtle,—who is so worthy to partake of these good things of life as the men who raise the beef and mutton and who ought to hunt the deer and the hare, and shoot the partridge and pheasant so long as they are to be hunted and shot; who catch the salmon and turtle and bring them to the market; we mean the working classes, who have to put up with coarse fare while idlers eat the whole of the food they produce. This is the sort of Free Trade we want. That one-sided middle-class Free Trade only made the rich richer, and the poor poorer. It ruined hundreds of little industries and hundreds of thousands of little men. And it is the little people that make the wealth and strength of any country, just as :—

> "Little drops of water, little grains of sand,
> Make the boundless ocean, and the mighty land."

To be sure thousands of dealers and middlemen made

their fortunes, but that has only done harm to the country, because they are wealth-holders now, who prevent the spread of money among the little men. "Oh! but," say the apologists, "don't they employ the little men?" Yes, they do, but they do not give them a chance to really live. They hold the monopolies of trade and must keep up a certain position. Some are socially ambitious and imitate the aristocracy in their extravagance, but the money they squander, does not go into the hands of the little men, for the rich always deal with the rich, and the working classes are kept in a struggling state of dependence, and want of many of the comforts of life. An ordinary working man with a family is in trouble whenever he wants a coat, a pair of boots, or any other article of clothing for himself or his family. His wages are just enough for sustenance. There is no margin for anything else. This ought not to be. Every man who can and *will* do a thorough day's work ought not to want for any of the necessaries of life, and should have many of its luxuries. It has been mentioned with a sort of comic surprise that miners drink champagne and buy pianos—not that it is true—but why should they not? Why should the idlers drink the most pleasant stimulants and enjoy a monopoly of the best kinds of musical instruments? Why should miners be condemned to fourpenny ale and hurdy-gurdies, while those who hold pieces of parchment stating that the mines are theirs, though they never go down into them, have champagne and pianos?

CHAPTER VI.

Foreign Manufactures and British Industry.

BUT we shall, perhaps, be taken to task by a certain influential liberal journal of the West of England for our inconsistency, as we once were for speaking of the farmers as middlemen who grind down their labourers to starvation wages. The talented editor may say "Mr. Mitchell is the last man who should inveigh against middlemen making their way in the world, especially by the importation of foreign goods, when Mr. Mitchell himself has made his money by importing Belgian marble work, which has not benefitted the mechanic in any way." We anticipate the objection by the reply that we are obliged to get on in the best way we can. If our people throw up their caps for Free Trade, and the free importation of manufactures becomes law, and if our customers will have the foreign goods, what are we to do? Besides, if we did not live up to our principles, which we do, so far as we can; if they are true, then our inconsistency will not alter their value. We are but mortal—our principles if they are based on justice, are immortal. Of one thing we are sure—we have no men working for us at starvation wages. We would rather that the absence of foreign competition compelled all employers to pay higher wages, for then we could raise prices in proportion, but in the face of all competition we *do* pay living wages. This one-sided Free Trade is wrong—we have no doubt about that, and the working classes have to suffer for it; but strange to say the very men who have to make pecuniary sacrifices for Free Trade do so cheerfully. They believe in it as a political religion and will scarcely hear the arguments of the other side. This is very foolish of our party, and is one of the weak points of the Liberals, because in reality there is no political principle involved in Free Trade at all. Free imports of corn were, no doubt, necessary to supply the food of the people, seeing that the population was increasing and the supply of corn could not increase, but the policy of Sir Robert Peel, rash as it was, and much as it has injured the poor farm labourers, was nothing like so injurious to the workmen of this country as that of Richard Cobden, who preached the doctrines of Free Trade in everything, with such success, that the majority of our working classes are his converts and are willing devotees to his cause. They praise him as their political saviour and benefactor, and then, when they find where the shoe pinches, they send a Trades Union delegate to remonstrate with employers of labour about the mischief they are doing to mechanics in importing foreign goods!

"But surely," say the true believers in second class Manchester liberalism "you would'nt dream of returning to protection?"——"Well, thereby hangs a tale" say we. "If the conditions of agreement between capital and labour are more easily adjusted under the reign of protection than of Free Trade, then return to ad-valorem duties—*if you can.*"

If a man has been giving away money to other people who have made him no return, if he has been doing business at no profit, or at a loss, with those who have been fleecing him in every possible way—if he has been generous to all the world, while all the world has been mean to him, and he finds at last it doesn't pay, and that the longest purse will get empty at that game, does it seem so very impossible or even improbable that he should turn round and say "Now I must draw in my horns?" and though his neighbours may cry "That's impossible!—after all these years of open-handedness, you can't be close-fisted now," he would very reasonably rejoin "I find I must—and depend on it I shall, and will, unless you show some spirit of reciprocity, unless in dealing with me you follow my example in dealing with you."

England, in like manner might well address the nations of the earth thus :—

"I, John Bull, was once doing a thriving business, and was regarded as manufacturer-general to the universe. So good was my name and so excellent were my profits that I said with the Psalmist "My mountain stands strong, I shall never be moved," and when those enterprising clerks of mine, Peel and Cobden, Bright and Gladstone, began to develope a loose, wide, competitive trade, instead of a snug monopoly such as I had for years enjoyed, in spite of many misgivings, I, like an old fool, gave way to their specious representations, and fondly listened to their rhapsodical ravings about Free Trade uniting the whole world in a bond of brotherhood. I was willing to throw out a sprat to catch a herring, but I have had to throw away my herring and have never yet caught the sprat. I find, according to my Blue Books, that I am doing an enormous business, that my exports and imports are very large, but I fail to find in my private ledger and balance sheets, the old profits. My workpeople too, though receiving higher wages than they were, are not so well off as in the old days, because the prices of all *necessaries* have risen faster than have their wages. Employment does not increase with the population, hence I have to draft off the best of my young men every year to enrich your lands with their labour. Pauperism has so increased that I have to enlarge, extend, and erect new workhouses everywhere. The end of it is, I shall now put my foot down, and when I, John Bull, do this, it is a firm foot, and will take some lifting, Henceforth I cannot afford to receive your manufactures duty free, unless you agree to the principle of RECIPROCITY. I will no longer be such a fool as to receive your wares without a contribution to my expenses, while you persist in laying 50 per cent. *ad valorem* duties on mine. Therefore, be it known unto all whom it might concern, that I, John Bull, have instructed my clerks to prepare a new schedule, the essence of which is—'All raw material to be received duty free, and to be exported free to those countries from whence they come untaxed. All manufactured goods to be taxed according to a sliding scale of the value of the labour, as compared with the raw material employed, and the proportionate taxation of other nations. Such duty to be entirely remitted in favour of reciprocal countries.' While insisting upon reciprocity, however, I desire my agents to encourage real Free Trade in every way, and to invite you to participate in that Free Trade through the medium of Reciprocity."

We conclude with the following pregnant sentences from a late anti-Free Trade pamphlet, the tenets of which, though apparently conservative, may yet become the property of the Trades Unionists of this country who will one day find, as our republican friends across the Atlantic have found, that native industry is the wealth of a country and must be protected.

"We not only doubt that Free-trade as it is called, has been conducive to the increase of profitable trade since 1847, but we are firmly of opinion that one sided trade has been the only drawback to almost unlimited prosperity in England, and we believe that if we had compelled reciprocity, or continued on the old system of protecting British industry, our prosperity would have been something beyond all computation. If Free imports were the cause of our increase of trade, then our exports to foreign countries should have increased far more then they have, taking into consideration the vast amounts that have been sent by foreigners to our colonies; we, however, as a nation, seem to think because our business has increased, it has done so in consequence of a special given cause—and that cause Free imports.

It does not follow that a very large trade is at all times a prosperous one; on the contrary, it is frequently observed that a small but good trade has enabled many to retire with an ample competence, while a large and bad trade has brought many into the gazette; so that the larger our trade is, if it is not a profitable one, the sooner shall we go to the wall, whether as individuals, or a nation.

It is true that the wealth of a certain favored few of the people of England is so enormous that it may be impossible to exhaust it, and that, as a whole, the wealth of England can bear any amount of losses; but, unfortunately, losses when they occur, fall not on these favoured few with the enormous wealth, but on the struggling many, and these are the working bees of the hive; the industry of this class is consequently paralized by want of success, and the result is that loss of money and emigration wind the matter up, so far at least as they are concerned." *

It may be asked what the Free Trade question has to do with the Farm Labourers, for we desire to pen the contents of this book chiefly, if not exclusively, in their interests. The reply would be, that whatever laws operate against labour, operate more especially against agricultural labour, for as the cultivation of the soil was the primary occupation of man, so it is the last resort of industry; both for the retired mechanic whose ambition is to invest his savings in a plot of land, and for the ruined lace-maker, art-workman or otherwise, who has been crowded out of trade by foreign competition, and who makes a pilgrimage to the hay or harvest-field to seek for work when it is plentiful, thus entering into injurious competition with the fielder in *his* harvest time and ultimately lowering his wages.

On the other hand, the rural districts are nurseries of

---

* " Free Trade a gigantic mistake " by JAMES ROBERTS.

labour from which all trades can be supplied with hands, and if trade increased in the same proportion as the population, that is to say, if trade, remunerative to the workmen as well as to the middle-men, increased with the increase of hands ready to labour, there would be a constant natural drain upon the supply of farm labourers, which would render them of more value, thus, whatever has tended to drive work in any department of industry, from our shores, to France, Belgium, Germany, and many other European countries, and also to America has helped to depress poor Hodge.

We therefore present the Free Trade question in its true light after a quarter of a century of consideration and experience, and we leave our readers to judge whether the middle-class Cobdenite party have, or have not assisted to reduce to a state of bones the Skeleton at the Plough.

CHAPTER VII.

JOHN BULL, LICENSED DEALER IN BEER, CIDER, WINE, SPIRITS AND TOBACCO. TO BE DRUNK ON THE PREMISES.

OUR ungentle readers (for the gentle ones have not, of course, been impatient) may begin to ask when we are coming to the history of the Farm Labourer's movement in the West of England? Just so—that's precisely what this little volume is to present to the public, but there are so many supplementary questions all bearing upon the main topic, that we are obliged to touch upon them as we go, on the principle of a crown advocate who not only proves that a murder has been committed, and who was the perpetrator, but demonstrates the motives and circumstances leading up, or rather down, to the crime. We have discovered the skeleton, the ghost has revealed to us the secret, but we have to prove to the jury of public opinion; who are the murderers, by what motives they were actuated, and what circumstances surrounded the crime.

Now, one of the alleged weaknesses of the Farm Labourer, oft quoted by bishops, aristocrats and parsons as the cause of his poverty and degradation, is a love of drink. Strange to say, it is generally at agricultural dinners, where the champagne flows so freely, that the poor diluted stimulants consumed by Friend Hodge are denounced in true Pecksniffian style by the reverend and noble guzzlers who knowing that the "agitators" have proved them "verily guilty concerning their brother," endeavour to make two wrongs one right, by blaming the victims of their selfishness for doing that which they are driven to do by shameful oppression and wrong.

Of course, it is very foolish of the men to take to drinking as some of them unfortunately do. Not that they have more than a penny or two to spend, and *that* is squeezed out of food for themselves and family, but they have been so accustomed to depend upon beer or cider for support in their prolonged toil, that when the little barrels or big bottles they carry to the fields are empty, they are lost men until they are supplied with more drink. They are not responsible for this—the farmers have encouraged them from their infancy to drink, as a part of their apprenticeship to the business—their bony frames have become habituated to carry an apology for a body, stimulated with the lowest class of fermented liquids, and so long as the ball is kept rolling, they can keep going, but like the Chinamen with their opium, once stop the supply, and they become, "of all men the most miserable."

Then their dwellings are, as a rule, so utterly unfit for human habitation, that men who have been labouring all day in the open air cannot possibly endure the close atmosphere of their unsavoury hovels,—damp, earthy, stifling—their half-starved wives rendered fiendish in temper by unending privations, alternately scolding the men for some imaginary wrong and savagely beating the children. Well, the poor fellows allow themselves to be driven out of doors, and where are they to go? They naturally seek the cozy sanded parlour of the nearest beer-house, where they fall in with companions in misfortune, and they manage to delude themselves for an hour or two into the belief that life is just worth having.

Of course, they are doing wrong—they cannot afford the two-pence for the pint of miserable swipes or sour cider, since it represents a tithe of their family income—they are in reality increasing their poverty, they are making matters at home worse and worse, they are in mortal fear of the parson, lest he should take cognizance of their nocturnal gaieties and they go drearily and dreamily to their work next morning with a sense of having "done those things which they ought not to have done."

But is it, generally speaking, wrong for men to spend their evenings in public places of resort, where beer, wine and spirits are retailed? "Peers, women, and parsons," (as the late Mr. Winterbotham said) will very probably answer "Yes." Well then—why are such places specially licensed by the government?

It is one of the most striking of the many hypocrisies of this country that society in general has a great horror of drink, and yet society guzzles the whole evening long—society affects to dislike public-houses, and yet the most expensive hotels are always crammed with what is called the cream of the cream of fashion—society affects to despise the publican, and yet gratefully accepted his assistance in forming a conspiracy to upset a progressive government, that had dared to restrict him a little in his much abused traffic, and the chief business of a whole session of parliament was to give an extra half-hour to the despised ones in which to retail their poisons, in short, the united kingdom is now in the hands of publicans—England has become one vast groggery—John Bull has become a publican in fact, and is, in the language of the rural sign-boards, licensed to sell beer, cider, wine, spirits and tobacco," inviting all his customers, as we think, most improperly " to be drunk on the premises."

CHAPTER VIII.

A FEW MORE WORDS ABOUT BEER, CIDER, WINE, SPIRITS AND TOBACCO.

THE ancient bishop of Bath and Wells, who wrote the first known drama in the English language, "Gammer Gurton's Needle," also composed a song upon the beer-drinking habits of the poor people of his diocese, the chorus of which runs thus—

> "Back and sides go bare, go bare,
> Feet go shiv'ring and cold,
> But belly, God send thee good ale enough,
> Jolly good ale and old."

so that it seems we were a beery race long before Shakespeare, who frequently demonstrated the large capacity for imbibation possessed by Englishmen, whom he proved to be "so potent at potting."

Now it is a moot point whether it is better to drink intoxicating liquors or not—We think *not* in the case of those persons who lead sedentary lives and have plenty to eat. We strongly recommend the upper classes to embrace teetotalism, especially should the bishops do so, as an example to the clergy, many of whose noses *do* "bring forth the fruits of good living" with a vengeance. As to curates, they ought to be prohibited by ecclesiastical law, the use of any stronger drinks than cowslip wine and cherry brandy. Their heads are evidently not constituted to stand any but the mildest of beverages. But no, while we are upon beer we might allow them a little single X—say half a tumbler twice a day, after matins and vespers, for of course, the regulation curate of the present day would'nt talk of anything so protestant as morning and evening service. Quite right too. Protestantism robbed the farm labourers of their land, and therefore, we shall not blame Nemesis for destroying established and endowed protestantism whenever she will.

But we digress—we were talking of beer—Well, are we to drink beer or not? Echo answers *not*, but the English people say otherwise and are ready to

Anathematise
Them chaps as tries
To rob a poor man of his beer.

Nor can we affect surprise at the jealousy of the poor, at the bare idea of being robbed of any little comfort of life. How many a toiler, exhausted by a sultry summer morning's work, longs for beer-time. How many a poor widow, forced to work hard for her family in spite of a weak constitution and failing health, finds the welcome half-pint of beer the only remedy for that " sinking in the stomach " she suffers from.—No, we would not hinder the right and legitimate use of beer, but when Englishmen become slaves to it, sell their birthright for it, muddle their brains with it, starve their wives and children for it, and last of all, yield up the very government of the country into the hands of brewers and publicans, we almost feel disposed to curse the beer itself, rather than such men as Sir Wilfred Lawson, who would prevent John Bull being such a wholesale dealer in this beverage.

Then we must, of course, have something to say about cider. Our Somersetshire nativity and proclivities would ensure due attention to the cider question. For Somerset is *par excellence* the cider county. Londoners do not understand cider. They regard Devonshire and Herefordshire as the great cider counties, the former more especially. Now this error has arisen from the want of enterprise of our old neighbours, the apple growers and cider brewers of Somerset. MARTOCK IS THE MARKET FOR CIDER. We recommend that sentence to be rapidily conned over, and anybody who will repeat it perfectly three times in a second, shall have a handsome fine next Christmas.

London cider may be characterised as a manufacture, concocted from such ingredients as the following, and in something like the following proportions, namely:—

    Rough Cider   1 gallon.
    New River Water 20 gallons.
    Acetic Acid   1 pint.
    Moist sugar   7-lbs.
    Oil of Pine-apple * a sufficient quantity.

Rack into small casks and label in blue and red
    "Pure Devonshire Cyder."

But if the metropolitan public were allowed to have

---

* This oil, like many other flavouring essences, is made from various kinds of filthy refuse, by the fermentation of which, are produced peculiar varieties of etherial oils resembling Pine-apple, Raspberry, Strawberry, &c.

any genuine Somersetshire cider, we venture to say they would thoroughly appreciate it, especially in the summer months. It contains a fine natural acid, chemically designated malic acid, which is a great help to the digestive organs. It is also a pleasant and valuable substitute for lemon juice. so necessary in gout, scurvy and other cutaneous diseases.

But cider, again, is made a curse to the farm labourers of the West, by being forced upon them in lieu of wages. And then, it is a very inferior article, scarcely fit even for a skeleton's drinking, yet the farmer reckons it at a shilling per gallon, when he would not have the chance of selling such mere washings of the cider-press to other classes at any price at all.

We cannot stay to descant upon the decanter, but we may, perhaps, do an excellent service to the Church of England, by endeavouring to disestablish and disendow old port, so much in favour with elderly rectors.

Perchance it may surprise those clerical magistrates who grow gouty and severe upon this compound, to be told that the best of port is not pure wine, that there is no such fluid as port wine in the world! It is a cordial, prepared expressly for the English market by the Spaniards and Portugese, of which, Spanish and Portugese clarets of a rough and peculiar character, form a part,— sugar, brandy and coloring matter, (logwood) making up the strength and body so much admired.

Now we don't very well like to steal away the household gods of so many old-fashioned English gentlemen, personally a very good sort, without giving them a substitute, we therefore append a recipe which may be useful to those who would like a good astringent, fruity port, equal to wine of '34 or any other date.

Take of Claret, one bottle.

Loaf Sugar previously dissolved in boiling water.
Decoction of logwood,
French brandy, (if you can get any.)
} A sufficient quantity.

Sweeten, strengthen, and colour to taste. After a time pour off clear, or filter through blotting paper.

The wine, or rather the port, will be good or bad according to the quality of the claret and the brandy respectively.

We have no more space for wine, but as so much money is unnecessarily spent in a vinous compound, and as very much of that money is extracted from the land which ought to feed the agricultural labourers decently, we have submitted a recipe by which the same mixture might be concocted at a reasonable figure, so that something may be left for beef to stoke the engines of the human machines who get all this wealth out of the soil.

A word as to spirits—Real French Brandy, distilled from wine, is an article at once so scarce, and so valuable as a remedial agent, that it ought to be reserved exclusively for the use of the sick. It is a pity that any healthy person should drink it, and very few do, for the reputed French Brandy sold in New York alone, is more than all the wine lees of Europe could produce. A number of very smart screw-steamers are constantly employed in taking rectified Irish whiskey in casks to France to be flavoured, bottled, labelled " Brandy," and packed in French cases, which the self-same steamers convey to the English ports.

Rum is a useful spirit, when the best quality can be obtained, but as the government are large buyers, they get the pick of the market, and the article that finds its way to the public is of very inferior quality. Persons who fondly indulge a cold in the head with rum and butter, are feeding an incipient fever, and offending an already inflamed stomach. Since the government however, provide the finest samples of rum for our sailors, it is a pity they do not consider the wants of our agricultural labourers, who are exposed to all weathers in their daily task of feeding the country, while the blue jackets are condemned to useless inactivity, waiting for war, against which calamity they utter regulation prayers every Sunday.

Although whiskey has had its victims in Scotland Ireland and America, and the "women's whiskey war" has been heard of in England, it is not such a dangerous public enemy as GIN. All who know the true condition of "London labour and the London poor," must have observed the frightful tax upon industry imposed by this Moloch of the people, gin. It is somewhat strange that it should be so, considering that gin is the weakest, the least palatable, and the most medicinal of all the distilled drinks. Gin, like brandy, is in reality a very valuable medicine, with more specific qualities than the latter. If it were retailed in its pure state, it would be more regarded in this light, the public would not take such large doses, or with such frequency and regularity as they do, and they would then perhaps get to know when convalescence commenced and at what stage to leave off their medicine, whereas now, they are never out of the doctor's hands.

Summing up upon the liquor question, we would briefly say, that we are sorry for poor human nature, that any regulation of the spirit-traffic should be necessary. It is a hindrance to legitimate trade, that so useful a chemical as alcohol should be hampered with a tax of several hundred per cent. upon its value, and that citizens, quite as good as their neighbours, who happen to deal in this article, should be watched day and night to see what time they open and close their shops. We have no hesitation in saying that brandy, being an important remedial agent, should be as come-at-able in the night as any medicines sold by chemists, besides, why should we be prevented drinking, any more than eating, what we like?

It is well worthy of debate, whether we should stop the sale of intoxicating liquors, or suspend the liberty of those who habitually abuse them. We think the proposed "Permissive Bill" would have this good effect, discussion would be promoted upon this most important topic, and something would be done to prevent John Bull having so many of his customers complying with the last clause of his sign-board.

With regard to tobacco, it is a shame, when soldiers on foreign stations, and sailors, have this luxury free of duty, that our agricultural labourers and workmen generally, have to pay hundreds per cent. of taxation upon every ounce of weed they smoke. Besides this, the free importation of tobacco leaf would find employment for thousands of cigar makers, both male and female, and then we might get a cheap and good cigar like other nations do, while Ireland might become a second Cuba in wealth and celebrity for the growth of this foolishly overtaxed herb.

CHAPTER IX.

Gold Discovery, a Friend to the Rich, and an Enemy to the Poor.

WE don't hold a diploma of competence as currency doctor, but we have our notions about the effect of the gold discoveries of California and Australia upon the wages, provisions, and raw materials of this country.

It is well-known, and that by painful experience, to housekeepers of long standing, that the prices of provisions have risen enormously within the last twenty years, and there are certain foggy philosophers who have ascribed this phenomenon to "strikes," and the consequent rise in wages!

They say—" These working folks are no better off for their wretched strikes—for when they *have* gained an increase of wages, they only find that prices rise in the same proportion." We know a very clever man of science who wrote a pamphlet to prove that the rise of wages, *caused* the rise of provisions, and he appealed to the working classes not to be so selfish as they were, for in raising the prices of all the necessaries of life by their foolish desire to have more money in their hands on a Saturday, which would buy them no more food; they were raising those prices for persons who could not obtain an increased income, such as pensioners, annuitants, widows deriving their little means of living from the 3 per cents., and others, who were being more and more injured by these shameful strikes and augmented pay, and the advanced rates of the produce market.

Now it does'nt much matter what this kind of philosopher says at any time. As Byron said—

"When Bishop Berkeley said there was no matter,
  'Twas *no matter* what he said."

but unfortunately, there are many silly people who accept this kind of sham logic and repeat it until it gets to be a doctrine, like that of Free Trade, and then interested men, desiring to make an outcry against Trades Unions, will take up the cry and make use of it, ridiculous as it may be.

A farmer once observed to us that when wages were 6/- per week, beef was 6d. per pound, when they rose to 10/- beef was 10d. per pound; but he forgot that the fact that the two prices had risen together, did not prove that the one caused the other, it rather proved that there was some common cause for both. He might as well have ascribed the rise of beef to the Transit of Venus as to the rise of labourers' wages.

But what is the cause of this advance in prices of everything that one really wants, excepting bread? Why because a sovereign is not so valuable now as it used to be. What is a sovereign? Only a counter representing so much food, clothing or luxuries. Our favourite coin happens to be intrinsically valuable, but its only real use to those through whose hands it passes is its purchasing power. A greasy American five-dollar bill or Scotch one-pound note would do about the same work, so that after all, your pound is only worth what it will buy. Now gold, being the base of our currency, when measured by its own standard, has not fallen in price notwithstanding all the discoveries of California and Australia, because our government has dogmatised as to what the price of gold shall continue to be, (they might just as well have ordered the mercury in the thermometer to remain stationary.) But, measured by the standard of all the necessaries of life, it *has* fallen in price, and the general rise in provisions and raw material simply means *a fall in the price of Gold*. If gold had been allowed to follow the natural course of events, its value would have been depreciated. A sovereign is not worth more than 10/- now, as compared with the sovereign of forty years ago, certainly not in its food-purchasing power in the West of England.

Well, the farmer has had the benefit of this, because all his produce has fetched enormous prices; and the farmer is all the better for the gold discoveries because he has been able to match the Australian product with his agricultural produce and get plenty of the former in exchange for the latter.

Then the landlord, finding which way the cat jumped, regularly sent his Scotch steward to demand of the farmer some of his gains, which the farmer has had to yield up, and by this means, the nobility and gentry have gained considerably by the gold discoveries.

It may be asked "How are the landlords and farmers better off, if gold falls as prices rise?"

Why, they are just this much better off, that after you have purchased necessaries, your money will now go farther for luxuries than in the old times. Clothing is cheaper, too, so that whoever has a margin over actual food, can make a better appearance and live in a more civilized manner than before. The rich had always enough food—they have now become richer, and since food only represents a tithe of their expenditure, they do not with their vastly augmented incomes feel the increase in prices.

The farm labourer, on the other hand, in common with all the working classes have this advance of prices thrown upon them. Their wages have not kept pace with the value of provisions, and Trades' Unionism becomes necessary throughout the whole field of labour, to ensure the workman in the face of these changes, a fair day's wages for a fair day's work.

CHAPTER X.

THE CONDITION OF THE POOR FARM LABOURERS OF THE WEST, BEFORE THE DAWN OF UNION.

WE shall not content ourselves with merely describing the dreadful state of the Agricultural population before union agitation commenced, but will first bring the evidence of landlords, parsons, farmers, stewards and others, who could have had no motive for exaggerating the miseries of their humbler brethren, but on the contrary, had a direct interest in representing a state of affairs, for which they were, many of them, responsible, in as favourable a light as possible.

This evidence was collected, not by "agitators," but by aristocrats and gentlemen of legal and literary talent, employed by the government as commissioners, and the volumes from which we extract these particulars, are the Blue Books of Her Majesty's Commissioners of Enquiry on the employment of women and children in agriculture. The samples of evidence we copy from these ponderous tomes, are taken haphazard, just as a voyager might dip a bottle of the briny from the Atlantic. There are oceans of facts—Here are samples for the inspection of our readers.

As we are chiefly interested in Somersetshire, we will begin at the beginning of the Somerset division, and to show that we do not pick out the worst statements, but take them as we find them, we will begin with No. 1.

"Williton Union. Meeting of Board of Guardians at Williton, February 15th, 1869, the Rev. Robert Poole, vicar, in the chair. Present: Sir Peregrine Acland, Bart., Sir Alexander Hood, Bart., &c., &c.

"General sense of the Meeting as regarded boys--Boys employed very young, beginning first at 8 or 9, bird-keeping, but that is not regular work; it lasts for a few months, and then the boy leaves off work again, and can go to school if he or his parents wish it. In the present low state of the wages, parents cannot get on with a large family unless they send them out into the fields as soon as they are old enough to earn a shilling or two. The wages in the district are very low, but as the union extends from near Bridgewater to the Devonshire border, there is room for increase; thus, near Porlock the money wages are 7/- to 8/-, about Stowey, 10/-; farmers cannot afford to raise wages unless rents are lowered, and in the present state of eager competition for land, landlords are not likely to lower their rents. The consequence is, that to eke out the subsistence of a family, a child is sent to work as soon as he can earn anything, and by making 2/- to 2/6 by bird-keeping, he can support himself, free of expense to his parents. It is not the farmers who want them out so much as the parents; though on this subject accounts are contradictory, Mr. Corner, of Sampford Brett, one of the largest farmers in the union, said that the parents sent out their young children to oblige him

At the same time it is an object to a farmer to get his work done as cheaply as possible, and if he has a large farm, he will require many young bird-keepers; of course, the younger the child, the cheaper his labour. Bird-keeping is generally done by boys, but little girls are employed too, in some districts, just as frequently as boys. Bird-keeping has to be done all the week round; a boy cannot have a holiday from it on Sunday. *

"The gentlemen who presided did not at all approve any plan of preventing boys under 12 from working out; the general sense seemed to be that if that were done, the labouring classes could not get on. A sturdy boy of 11 wants more food and clothes than his father on 8/- a week can afford to give him, while he is living in idleness and making nothing towards the common purse."

"The Rev. Mr. Poole † said that compulsory education is a dream. You cannot introduce it unless government votes money to pay the parents for work the children might have done, had they been sent out to work early, instead of going to school, and to do that all over the country would require millions."

---

* Little boys and girls are thus shown to be kept all day long from dawn to dark, alone, in the wide fields in all weathers and all seasons, to earn a shilling or two a week to eke out the starvation wages paid to their strong, able-bodied fathers, whose increasing toil is used to maintain landlords, parsons and gentlemen farmers in grandeur, and not his own poor little children.

† The great anxiety of the clergy of the Church of England for the education of their parishioners is here seen. Surely the School Board is wanted in these districts.

"The women employed are mostly labourers' wives. It is often expected when a farmer lets a cottage to a labourer, that his wife should, if able-bodied, * go out to work. Their regular rate of wage is 8d. per day. Mr. Corner says that they are the cheapest kind of labour you can have; many of them will do almost as much as a man and their pay is half as much.

Dr. Trevor, of Dulverton says—

"Wages are little more than 8/- a week in money, with privileges, such as 3 pints of cider, run of a pig, † (sometimes on the road!) a bad cottage (not rent free) grist corn at 6/- a bushel, when at that, or a lower market price. If it is below the market price they generally have none left.

"Cottages are very bad in the district generally, specially at Withypool. Cider is not bad for the health; it is often given at Exeter hospital instead of wine, but that may be in consequence of an old tradition.

"Mr. Hardinge gives his labourers in the summer 7/- per week.

"Charles H. Fox, Esq., of Wellington, remarks— "Although the people live close on a railway, by which it would seem, that when discontented with their wages they might easily move elsewhere, *they are so helpless* that it never occurs to them to move, unless the way is made smooth for them by some one taking all the ar-

---

* A farmer will often ask to see the wife before he will employ the man, and if she be an amazon, the man will get the place, so that the master will obtain as good as two men's labour for 2s. per day.

† But he did not say where the pig was to come from.

rangements into his hands, and settling where they are to go. * Thus, though 12/- are to be earned within two hours railway of Milverton, where they only earn 8/-, they will not move on the chance of work. (What more need be said to show that a Labourers' Union was required?)

W. Ayshford Sanford, Esq., of Nynehead Court, said—"The most to be enquired into will be the Wiveliscombe district, on the slopes of Exmoor, where the people are very much in the hands of the farmers, getting in that part of the country only 7/- a week. (Wiveliscombe has since been pretty well enquired into) "Cottage property is a bad speculation; cannot build one under £100, or let it over £4 per annum, and that is no return for a landlerd who has to pay repairs out of the rent." (Yes, but who robbed the aborigines of their land? Why the landlords! And their descendants now talk of making good speculations out of mere dwellings for them)! "Would like to see a state of things where cottages could be let for £7, which would be a fair return, but to get that, the labourers' wages must be 14/- or 15/-. (Mr. Sanford is one of the most excellent and humane of the landlord class, yet his highest aspiration for the poor ploughman is fifteen shillings a week, in order that an aristocrat or a county-family man shall make 7 per cent. out of him.—"If

---

† Yet this self-same Mr. Fox, when we invited him to a meeting at Wellington, wrote us a very impolite note to the effect, that if we and other "agitators" came into his neighbourhood we should do more harm than good.

they do these things in the green tree, what shall be done in the dry?")

Statement of Mr. J. Lutley, occupier, Parsonage Farm, Wiveliscombe, which farm is entitled "Enclosure No. 1" (More common land taken from the people?) "An account of the money payments to my five farm labourers for the year 1867.

	£	s.	d.	
James Baker, day work	17	9	2½	
Task work	6	5	0	
	23	14	2½	about 9/1 per week.
Isaac Greedy, day work	19	16	3	
Task work	5	7	6	
	25	3	9	about 9/8 per week.
William Bale, day work	20	2	4	
Task work	2	15	8	
	22	18	0	about 8/9 per week.
Martin Baker, day work	20	4	2	
Task work	3	6	6	
	23	10	8	about 9/1 per week.
Henry Baker, day work	20	8	9	
Task work	1	16	4	
	22	5	1	about 8/6 per week.

Now, if we analyse this statement, we shall see that an attempt was made to prove that these men were earning 9/- per week, but if we add up the payments made for the day work of the men, we shall find that Mr. Lutley was commanding the daily labour of five strong men for £98 a year, just enough for one of them to live upon comfortably, as a hard-working man and his family should live!

Take the case of James Baker, the first-mentioned of the five, who was said to be earning 9/1 per week, his day work was acknowledged to fetch £17 9s. 2½d. in one year!

Now this only shows 6/8 per week! As the statement is that he earned 9/1 for day work, we suppose he got the other 2/5 for *night* work, and as to these phantom extras and perquisites, we don't believe in them at all now. Let the men have their wages (and every able-bodied farm labourer ought to be worth 4/- or 5/- a day to his employer at the least) and if the farmer thinks it to his interest to give men cider or beer in order to stimulate them to more than ordinary exertion, don't let ignorant people be any longer humbugged into the belief that it forms a part of the men's wages.

But this same Mr. Lutley is somewhat foggy on the subject of task work. He says, that James Baker obtained £6 5 0! How, in the name of conscience? when in the statement headed "Enclosure No. 2, he has a special calculation as follows—

"Extra Wages.

Harvest, say, on an average, 10 days carrying corn, 1/- extra each day, 10/-.

Turnip hoeing, generally three men only." (We suppose he means that only three men get extras for this duty.)

" Christmas Gifts (!)

In hay time, a supper (!)

Shepherds get 1/- a week extra."

(Now we don't see James Baker's £6 5 0 here, as the haymaking extras are only a supper, and as harvest-pay for overtime (sometimes till 10 or 11 o'clock at night) only amounts to 10/- we are bound to conclude, especially as the private information of the men confirms our surmises, that the 6/- or 7/- was the reality, while the wonderful task work and extras and perquisites were chiefly imaginary, especially when the feeding of a pig at the roadside is reckoned an extra, and the sale of light grist corn at 6/- per bushel, (not worth 5/- in the market), is called a perquisite.

The Rev. E. J. Carter, vicar of Kingston, testifies as follows :—

"Nearly all the women work in the fields. Men's wages 8/-. Many farmers in letting a cottage to a labourer stipulate that his wife is to work too. One farmer complained to him of a woman who was so lazy that she would not work in the fields ! another threatened to turn a whole family out of doors, because the wife, *who was in the family way,* would not work !"

A clergyman speaks of a child of five years of age as one of the working classes of his parish, and the whole sum of the matter is just this—the farmer is bound to pay a rising rent, and tries to keep a little money against the next notice from the landlord, so that he is obliged to screw down the labourer to such low wages, that his wife and family, even to the very babies have to turn out in all weathers to earn enough to eat.

CHAPTER XI.

The Romantic Cottages of the West, and the Rural Felicity Enjoyed by Our Friends in their "Homes."

CANON GIRDLESTONE, one of the few active friends of the Farm Labourer before the foundation of the Union, a man who would have been a bishop long ago, but that he offended the aristocracy by taking up the cause of the oppressed hireling in a truly scriptural manner, made use of the following memorable words in a speech at the Bath Church Congress in describing the cottages of the Agricultural Labourers; cottages he had visited and knew of his own knowledge, were nests of physical and moral disease; "cottages" he said "which were in too many instances hovels, in which not one of those present would consent to stable their horses—hovels without ventilation, drainage or the surroundings necessary for ordinary decency; hovels which bred a race of men who from want of domestic comfort spent their lives in the pothouse, and who had nothing to look forward to but to be buried in a pauper's grave!—hovels which bred a race of women whose maidenly blushes were blotched in consequence of the scenes they were obliged to witness through the want of proper sleeping accommodation."

The following extracts from the Blue Book before-mentioned, show that this was not an overdrawn picture.

WIVELISCOMBE, SOMERSET.

"A man, Samuel Greedy, wife and five children of whom the eldest is a boy of 15, and the youngest a baby; one boy is deformed: they have only one bed-room for the seven."

Mr. Lucas, schoolmaster said—

"The cottage accommodation is most demoralising. What can you expect from a father, and mother, three or four boys and two or three girls, all sleeping in the same room. I know a group of three cottages, with only one bed-room in each, containing 27 souls."

PORLOCK, SOMERSET.

"Mrs. Cook's cottage, only two rooms. Husband, wife, and seven children with only one bed-room."

The Revd. J. A. Miller, vicar of Isle Brewers, deposed—

"Some cottages are very bad and over-crowded, in consequence of which the tone of morality is low and no disgrace attaches to the birth of illegitimate children."

The Rev. Charles Southey, vicar of Kingsbury Episcopi, after giving evidence to the effect that wages were so low that boys of 5 and 6 had to work all the year round for their food, says—

"Many of the cottages are very bad; being let on

leases, and the poor people being unable to repair them, there is much overcrowding and immorality."

The Rev. Charles Leigh Pemberton, rector of Curry Mallett, says—

"The cottages are very bad. Some are overcrowded, and evil effects have followed. This is owing to the desire for increasing small wages by taking in lodgers. They are well ventilated *because they are so dilapidated!*"

"Henry Robertson, Esq., agent to Lord Taunton, "could show me some dreadful cottages, and the people live, very large families, in one room."

Let us now visit the "great dismal swamp" of Sedgmoor, with Her Majesty's Commissioner, to see the cottages at Edington Burtle, near Bridgewater, which he describes as follows—

"Miserable place in the middle of the swamp, best cottage, a Mrs. Cox, old lady in a wig. Had been built for the sexton. Close by, a mere hovel with open thatch and two very small windows, now a stable, where lived and died an old farm labourer."

"John Holly lives in half an old dilapidated cottage on the moor. Water comes up to the door in floods, and we had to jump two peat ditches to get there. They have a plank, but that had been removed. It has two rooms, one above and one below; in it live a father, mother, two big sons, daughter aged 19, with a child. The mother was out at work. A girl of 9 was kept at home to look after the baby."

"Richard Coombes has three boys at home, of whom the eldest is aged 15; two girls, eldest 13; only one room, divided by a partition and a blanket; very ruinous, rough-paved stone floor, thatched, with light visible through one place, built of hard sand, leaning forward and nearly tumbling down, kept together by laths. A wild, rough looking girl, *hardly clothed*, showed us the cottage."

At Bawdrip, in the same neighbourhood, we find—

"Mrs. Clist. Bad cottage, thatched, rough stone floor, rent 2/- per week. Seven children, husband a carter on 10/- a week."

"Mrs. Sellick. Reckoned the best cottage in the village. Rent £4 per annum, and pays rates and taxes. Has seven children. Husband, a labourer; gets 10/- a week, which is all the money that comes in."

"The Rev. E. Coney, vicar of Burtle says—

"The cottages are with few exceptions very bad. In the winter the lowlands are flooded, and then, cottages above high water mark are indecently over-crowded; the state of morality is low. All have not gardens, but most of the cottagers can rent potato ground at a high rate, £10, to £12 an acre." (About 6 times as much as farmers pay.)

The Rev. Giles Pugh, vicar of Shapwick says—

"Like the cottages of most other villages, they are small and overcrowded, but still the occupants take in lodgers whenever they can get them, and crowd them more. I cannot say whether immorality has arisen particularly from this cause, but there is a *low tone* prevalent, especially in Ashcott."

Then if we accompany the royal commissioner in his

"visit to Butcombe," near Axbridge, we shall find "another thatched cottage in which lived a man and wife and five children in one room. There were holes in the roof. In winter they have to move the bed about to escape the rain." Also " a family of 14, who live like rabbits, scarcely dressed, and if any one came into the village they would scurry away like rabbits to hide their nakedness!"

The Rev. William Hunt, vicar of Congresbury, declares—

"The number crowded together in a bed-room is most debasing, some young women over 13 and up to as old as 22, sleep in the same bed-room with their mother and father. In some cases *worse arrangements are made*. Modesty is destroyed and the whole tone of the mind lowered. I am sure much depravity exists from this source. In cases of sickness and death this is especially detrimental to health and comfort."

Rev. J. B. Archer, vicar of Churchill, speaks of "some wretched cottages which depend for water entirely on the brook into which their sewerage falls. When fever comes, they look upon it as the hand of God."

Rev. Charles Dimsdale says—

"The cottages in this parish are mostly huts, no better than stables, and some are so filled, that it is impossible that morality and decency can exist."

The Rev. A. Goldney, vicar of East Pennard says—

"In some cases the cottage accommodation is very bad, both sexes and all ages being mixed together in one bed-room," and the rev. gentlemen adds "The moral effect is bad."—We should rather think it was.

The Rev. John Davies, vicar of Ashwick, speaks of—

"Cottages bad, with large families and only one bed-room," and he says, "the population has gone down one fourth since 1840."

The Rev. W. J. F. Edwards, vicar of Stoke Lane, says—

"Bed-room accommodation is very bad; many, with only one bed-room. Birth of illegitimate children not thought such a disgrace as it ought to be."

Mr. Bird, relieving officer, Wincanton, says—

"Cottages in some parts of the district are bad, and there is a good deal of overcrowding, chiefly owing to the admission of lodgers; immorality naturally follows."

The Rev. Canon R. Meade, Castle Carey, in speaking of the cottages in his district, observes—

"Some have too many occupants. I can hardly specify immorality as a direct result, but overcrowding must have that tendency."

The Hon. and Rev. W. Portman, Corton Denham, says with regard to the cottage accommodation of his parish—

"There is overcrowding in some instances. . . . The crowding of young persons together in cottages is not conducive to morality, but sometimes a large crowded family turns out well, sometimes the reverse. As to health, it seems to make little difference. All that are crowded, are crowded with family,"—by which foggy sentence we suppose the Hon. and Reverend Gentleman means, that, however large the family, they have to lie in one room, and their health, moral, and physical, is a matter of chance. But does it never occur to gentlemen who are Honourable as well as Reverend, that they might use their influence to put a stop to this state of things?

The Rev. William Castlehow, rector of North Cadbury, says of his parish—

"The cottages are generally bad, some overcrowded, and several cases of immorality in consequence, have come under my notice."

"Dr. Marsh, of Nunney, reports that the condition of the cottages in Nunney is bad. There are many very small, with only two rooms and much crowded. Cannot say, however, that ill health is produced, except in times when there was an epidemic going about. The parish is morally in a very bad state. Know several instances of men living with other men's wives, and the proportion of illegitimate children is very large. The bad moral state to be attributed to the crowding in the cottages, and the want of visiting,—for the rector never visits."

Rev. Charles Foster, rector of Compton Martin says—

"The cottages are very bad; the squire never repairs them, but lets them go to ruin, while he turns out any one who improves on his own account."

Rev. Mark Warburton, rector of Kilmington says—

"The cottages are bad, neglected alike by landlord and tenant; rent high and accommodation small; walls and floors in a ruinous condition, and sadly wanting in cleanliness."

The Rev. E. A. Salmon, vicar of Martock, reports—

"In a cottage containing one living and one bed-room, about 11-feet square each, there lived together I.M., and E.M., man and wife; V.M., and L.M., man and wife, (nephew of above); M.A.M., un-marrried woman, (daughter of I.M.); and her three illegitimate children, aged about 18, 10 and 5 respectively; and sometimes another man, (son of I.M.,) sleeps there also."

"Man and wife and 4 children 17 to 12—boys and girls sleeping in same bed."

"Numerous cases of young men and girls sleeping in one room."

William Sturge, Esq., land agent, Bristol, writes to the Commissioner as follows—

"Cottage accommodation is generally bad in the Western Counties, deficient in bed-rooms, repairs and draining."

"In reply to the question 'Have you any remarks to make on the subject of cottage accommodation?' the gentlemen who have filled up circulars are almost of one mind in complaining of the cottage accommodation of Somersetshire."

At the monthly meeting of the Dorchester Farmers' Club, on Saturday, January 30th, 1869, Dr. Aldridge, F.R.C.S. said—

"With respect to cottages, there were some in that neighbourhood very bad, some belonging to their best landed proprietors. He knew a cottage not half so large as the room they were in, without ceiling or floor and containing 8 or 10 persons, with a window certainly, a foot square, but without the possibility of being opened, the consequence being fever among the inmates. In Fordington, the cottages were very bad. He ventured to say they would not fatten their animals in such places,—they would think them too bad even for that—and yet they were occupied by families of five or six individuals. In many of these cottages one could not stand upright, and the smoke, dirt, and filth altogether made a state of things not to be equalled in St. Giles' He thought it high time that some notice should be taken on this matter."

"A large amount of *fatal diseases* has been for many years the deplorable consequences,—in fact, Fordington has been a hot-bed for the generation of the most frightful phases of disease.—Cholera, small-pox, typhus and typhoid fevers have many times almost decimated the parish, as a consequence of the filthy and wretched dwellings of the poor."

The Rev. Lord Sidney Godolphin Osborne, (the celebrated S.G.O. of the "Times,") says—

"I could point to a few notorious localities where the state of the dwellings of the poor is disgraceful to humanity," and adds "so long as estates can be tied up for generations, loaded with settlements and so parchment-hampered that the proprietors are such, far more in name than in fact, society at the same time expecting them to live up to the standard of their supposed proprietorship, it is clear that estate improvement is out of the question."

We have no more space for this topic, but say in conclusion, and without fear of contradiction, that bad as the foregoing evidence shows the homes of our farm labourers to be, it does not present a tithe of the real state of wretchedness in which they exist.

CHAPTER XII.

The Educational Status of the Farm Labourers, How they Live, and the Enlightenment of our Rural Parishes.

THE Hon. E. Stanhope, records in his Blue Book, an account of a meeting at Blandford, Dorset, where, as Assistant Commissioner, he met the Guardians of the Poor to confer with them. He specially notes that "In the discussion which took place one of the guardians deprecated any interference. '*The less education labourers have, the better.*' Whenever a boy can earn 2/- he ought to go to work. Some of his best men were uneducated. There was a school in the parish to which he did not subscribe as he considered it a landlord's question.' These remarks were received with some applause, and a discussion took place, during which, the effect of education in withdrawing children from agricultural work was remarked on, and compulsory school attendance and rates were strongly condemned."

This feeling on the part of the guardians is quite

sufficient to account for the ignorance of the great mass of the Western Farm Labourers at that time, the majority of whom could neither read nor write, as the parish records will witness, in the large number of crosses or marks in lieu of signatures at weddings. Girls who could write, would sometimes pretend they could not, because they would'nt out-do their newly acquired husbands in knowledge, and make them feel their inferiority, and they would also make their "criss-crass" to match the men's marks.

Fortunately, since the union agitation and the institution of school-boards, though they are merely permissive and do not exist everywhere, something in the direction of public Education has been done, but we are yet only on the threshold of duty in this direction, and very much more has to be done; while the culpable neglect of landlords and parsons of the past generation is painfully apparent in the gross ignorance of many of the labourers of the present day,—instance the fact, that when some men in the neighbourhood of the city of Wells, only a few months ago, had to sign an agreement, they not only could not sign their names, but had no idea whatever of making the usual mark, so that the farmer had to guide their hands to form a cross.

But let us see what was the mental and moral condition of the rural people at the time of Mr. Boyle's commission in 1869.

The schoolmistress at St. Audries says—"Boys are taken away altogether at about 9 to work about the farm."

Dr. Trevor, of Dulverton, says of the labourers of his neighbourhood—

"I can quite believe Canon Girdlestone's story of the people he sent to Yorkshire, asking whether they had to cross the sea to get there!

"The state of morality is very low. It is all very well for women to be afraid of sending their boys to towns, but there is quite as much temptation for them in the country. . . A short time ago a woman of 35, came to the Union to be confined of a child by her uncle, and did not seem the least ashamed of the connection. Some time ago a proposal was made, with a view to checking this evil, that all women who came to be confined of an illegitimate child, should wear spotted gowns instead of striped. The late Lord Fortescue and other men of influence took it up, and a special meeting of the Guardians was held to consider the subject. One of the farmer-guardians, however, got up and said that if this were done, it would be only just that the fathers should wear spotted jackets too, and winked at some of the younger ones, so the affair went off with a laugh and nothing was done."

Another version of the same story says, that when the proposal for the spotted jackets was received, a farmer exclaimed "What a show of spotted clothes there would be on a board day!"

We should not quote such stories as these, which disclose immoralities horrible to contemplate, but they are in the Blue Book, reported by Her Majesty's Commissioners, and we are bound to represent things as they were, in order to show the imperative necessity which existed for some interference with a system of degrading and demoralising serfdom, scarcely better than negro slavery in any sense, and worse in the matter of food.

Nor do we for one moment mean to imply that all farm labourers were ignorant and immoral, since we happen to know that there were, and are, very many farm labourers, who, with their wives and daughters, were, at that time, as now, highly respectable people—but then they must have been a sort of elect or special remnant, inspired from above with graces and virtues exemplary to all mankind, or they never could have kept their heads above the general flood of degradation and demoralization around them.

But then these highly respectable farm labourers are very simple people—ignorant of the ways of the world. A wife, apparently of this class, in giving her evidence before the commissioner, after detailing her poverty and frugality and her struggles to make both ends meet, says—

" I never had anything from the parish in my whole life. My husband was ill about a fortnight, and the doctor's bill was £7 1 0! We paid it by degrees."

Now this medical gentleman, whoever he was, could not have made such a demand as this upon educated people. He would not have attempted to charge the rector of the parish half that amount for a fortnight's attendance, and this is why we echo the cry of " Education for the Poor! School Boards for ever!" because we plainly see that while education is confined to any class, it will be used as a means of screwing money out of the ignorant, We don't know the name of this sharp practitioner, nor do we wish to, we should call him Dr. Skinflint, but were we Grand Vizier of his district for half an hour, we would compel him to swallow a little of his own physic, as the worst punishment we could inflict upon such a human leech who attempted to bleed a stone.

The Rev. Alexander Tate vicar of King's Brompton speaks of two schools in his village as—

"One a dame's school, and one an infant school. The main causes of irregular attendance are the truant disposition of the children and the extreme indifference of the parents on the subject."

The Rev. F. King Warren, rector of Exton, speaking of the boys of his parish, says—

"Their pay is only 2d. or 3d. a day, which hardly pays for wear of clothes. Farmers are beginning to think, too, that if there is not a man to watch a boy he does no work. They object rather to education. One said the other day that the boys knew more than the farmers. There is a dame's school in the parish."

The Rev. Joseph Jekyll, of Hawkridge, says—

"I have a dame's school at Hawkridge, and had a day school at Withypool, from 1836 to 1856, which was very well attended. The farmers subscribed to it at one time, but as soon as their own children were educated, withdrew their subscriptions and left me to support the school, which I was obliged to give up for want of means."

The Commissioner adds—

"There are a good many dissenters there, and they

got up a school and asked Mr. Jekyll to join. He said he would if they would teach the church catechism, but they declined, and so he would have nothing to do with it. Considers Withypool an immoral place."

Mr. Lucas, schoolmaster of Wiveliscombe, thus speaks of female field labour and its effects—

"They lose their delicacy which is followed by a loss of chastity; young lads become old in immorality; of all employment it is the worst for the union of the sexes. It undermines the health of the mother of a family, tramping the wet fields, digging the frozen roots for the sheep, weeding, &c. The old coat or jacket of the husband is coming much in vogue. It hardens the finer feelings of the women, they neglect home duties, their children roam the roads and fields unkempt and uncared for. The older children nurse the younger, dwarfing their stature, damping their vivacity, by the care devolving on them, besides the detriment to the younger from bad nursing, and long hours without food. Till the wages of the labourers are raised, I cannot see how, with a family, her earnings, (6d. or 8d. per day) can be dispensed with. What are 7/- or 8/- for a family? It will barely suffice for bread. One penny for each meal, and three meals a day is little enough. I would prohibit female labour altogether except in harvest. Education is in my opinion perfectly thrown away, when there is no parent to carry it on at home. Tired, jaded, perhaps her washing to do; what can you expect from a woman? (!)" The note of admiration, in a parenthesis, is the Commissioner's, not ours, who adds, speaking of the same place " There are 100 to 150 children, quite uneducated, owing to the apathy of their parents, chiefly."

C. Smith, Esq., Bishop's Lydeard, says—

"The state of morality in the parish and neighbourhood generally, is bad. Mr. Smith complains that many affiliation cases come before him, some very bad ones, women in their employment, having children by young farmers. In a neighbouring parish a girl of 15 gave birth to a child and swore it on a boy of her own age." *

Henry John Pearce, relieving officer, Bishop's Lydeard says—

"There are scores of illegitimate children in the district. Lydeard St. Lawrence is the worst. This place is bad."

Here follow many sickening recountals by relieving officers, of the squalid poverty, the overcrowded hovels, the bastardy and general degradation of the magnificent valley of Taunton Dean, a paradise of rich scenery, rich soils, rich gentry, rich parsons and rich farmers, but a pandemonium of pauperism, squalidity and immorality among the toiling population.

Dr. Wills, of Crewkerne, speaks of the immorality of his district, caused by overcrowding and ignorance.

The Rev. G. O. Mullens, of Chedzoy, says—

"The girls going out to work, they get about with the

---

* The relieving officer remarks on this case, that the girl's family lived in one room—father, mother, and five children, girls and boys aged 16, 14, 10, 8, and 6 years respectively.

men and learn to say things they hardly know the meaning of at first."

The Rev. R. Lambert, curate of Wells, says—

"In his parish of 2000, he believes that five out of eight children are illegitimate, which he puts entirely on female agricultural labour, the farmers setting the bad example themselves; one instance a farmer, and Mr. Lambert's own churchwarden, *and not at all ashamed of it.*"

Rev. Chas. Dimsdale of Priddy, where over 80 women are employed in agricultural labour, says—

"I think that females working mixed with the opposite sex is bad for their morals, manners and language, and begets rudeness and coarseness.

"About 40 children are employed. Bad weather seriously affects the attendance in this scattered parish, the people cannot afford to send more than two thirds of their children on an average through poverty."

The Rev. John Hickley, rector of Walton, says—

"Boys begin work very early, often at 7, even earlier in some instances. The parents are so poor that the extra money is a very great object to them. In the face of rents increasing with the demand for land, it is very difficult for wages to rise, the only means by which they could, would be a combination among the labourers, * but that never occurs to them; they are a stupid, down-trodden race, and then they have not

---

* Thus it is seen that the aspiration of a right-minded country clergyman in 1869, was towards the very Union, which has become an accomplished fact.

the same opportunities of meetings enjoyed by people in the towns, who can combine and form Trades Unions. They are still very superstitious. The custom of roasting a cat alive when anyone is supposed to be bewitched, has not gone out. Recollects at a funeral seeing a bystander throw a handkerchief holding bread and cheese on the coffin, when he came to the passage 'deliver us from evil.' It is supposed to be a cure for the king's evil."

The above evidence is upon the same page as that of the Rev. F. Philpott, of Chewton Mendip, and once in a speech, we accidentally quoted the passage on witchcraft as belonging to Chewton Mendip, whereupon the Rev. Mr. Philpott wrote a most indignant denial to the Wells Journal, but as we happened to know Chewton Mendip very well, and are, apparently, better acquainted with the manners and customs of the Chewtonians than the parson himself, we hereby give evidence that we know of our own knowledge that a belief in witchcraft was not at all uncommon at that time, in the village of Chewton Mendip, and as the nursery rhyme says :—

"There was an old woman lived under the hill,
And if she's not gone she lives there still."

The Hon. and Rev. W. Portman, speaks of :—

"Boys and girls growing up with insufficient education, at school very irregularly. Read and write very badly. Girls and young women will not learn anything. The parent's means are so small that they remove the children who can earn anything."

The Rev. A. D. A. Burney, curate of Gaer Hill—

"Knows a child of 5 who goes out to hold horses, and a boy of 6 years, birdkeeping, picking stones, &c., When he asked a woman why she did not send a boy of 7 to school, she said she found him useful at home; haymaking, gardening, &c.

"Nearly all the women in the parish, work in the fields, more or less; some of them get a winter's work, and a summer's work; they become thoroughly degraded, working with the men and often doing a man's work; and meantime their families and homes go to ruin."

"The young women are very immoral; from 15 to 16 they take the summer work, and after that life, are not inclined to settle down into service or regular work. They go out late at night, and the mothers resent it if Mr. Burney interferes. Nearly half the children are illegitimate."

Rev. C. Foster rector of Compton Martin, says—

"The children are taken away very early to work, and forget everything."

"Mr. Foster considers that the chief signs of the degradation that prevails in this valley are that the people see no use in education and believe in witchcraft. If anyone has a fit, or the cow gives no milk, they consider they have been 'overlooked' (by the evil eye of a witch) and send to the wise woman of Bristol."

"The older people are utterly uneducated, and do not see why the children should be better off than themselves."

The Rev. E. P. Vaughan, rector of Wraxall, says—

"This is rather a pattern parish, as several rich people live here (the Gibbs') and take care of it. Yet there are families who never send their children to school. He thinks it runs in families; there is an apathy about it; the parents never learnt themselves and do not see the good of it."

With all due deference to the opinion of Mr. Vaughan, respecting "the Gibbs' pattern parish" we think the School Board would take much better care of the education of Wraxall than any rich Gibbses or anybody else.

In the answer to Commissioner's circulars, on the number of young persons growing up with insufficient education, we find that the Rev. J. L. Carrick, states that "in his parish (Witham Friary), there are many young men and women unable to read or write at all, and ignorant of the most ordinary matters."

The Rev. E. A. Salmon, Martock, knows 40 males and 110 females in his parish who "cannot read a chapter in the Bible or write intelligibly, and know nothing of arithmetic."

Rev. Chas. Sainsbury, of Wooton, states that a large proportion of his parishioners can neither read nor write.

In answer to further questions on education, the Rev. J. N. Garland, of Shipham, says—

"Many do not take advantage of the School from the carelessness of their parents, who, not having had the advantages of education themselves, care not to have it for their children."

Rev. J. N. Robinson, North Petherton, says in effect that there is no education after a boy can earn anything.

"Home duties interfere with the girls' education."

Rev. H. Roberts, Othery. Education of boys, "prevented by early labour and indifference on the part of parents."

Rev. J. W. Moor, Othery, speaks of "distance of schools, bad roads, and apathy," as causes of ignorance in his parish, and adds—"Farmers have a good deal to do with children not coming to school, and they will not subscribe."

Rev. J. A. Miller, Isle Brewers, says—

"There are several who either do not attend, or attend very irregularly. Some parents are utterly indifferent, and their children are much left to themselves—with an ignorant jealousy of interference on the part of the more ignorant parents, who have no idea of school discipline, and who, therefore, resent the punishment of their children, although they will often themselves half kill them, when offended with them."

Rev. C. C. Southey, Kingsbury, says—

"The people are indifferent to education; can hardly keep children at school after 8."

Rev. J. H. Evans, Merriott—"Many children are kept from school through the ignorance and poverty of their parents."

The Rev. J. M. Hawker, of Ideford, speaks of some of his parishioners, thus: He says—

"They are, for the most part, in a state of appalling ignorance."

But why should we waste good paper by further defacing it with records of the mental and moral degradation of the poor Farm Labourers of the West? It is well-known that the majority of the last generation of Farm Labourers could neither read nor write, and scarcely any of the middle-aged men of the present day are educated.

The prevalence of belief in witchcraft in the West of England is well-known to those who have lived in Somerset, Devon, and Cornwall. As to Somerset, we know of our own knowledge that such cases as the following, were, and are now, common in Somerset and Devon, old women being frequently wounded for no other reason than that they were suspected of having bewitched somebody, and caused them fits, pains or losses.

This case came before a full bench of magistrates at Weston Super Mare, in the year of Grace, 1874, the report of which we append:—

"HESTER ADAMS was summoned for assaulting Maria Pring, at Lympsham, on December 21.—Complainant stated that on the day in question, defendant came to her house and stabbed her in the hand and face, drawing blood—to prove whether she was a witch—and exclaiming, 'Now I'm happy now I have stabbed you.' Blood flowed from her face and hands. Witness did not tell people's fortunes,—In reply to the Bench, witness said she had never been served like it before, but defendant had threatened to stab her in the presence of Mr. Stephenson.—Defendant: I can prove that she is an old witch, and she have hag-rided me and my husband for the past two years. The Bench: In what way?—Defendant: She comes to my house and groans at me. I have often seen her in the night.—The Bench: Do you believe she has an evil eye?

Defendant: I know she is an old witch.—The Bench: What do you mean by calling her a witch?—Defendant: Why, an evil spirit.—The Bench: Why do you not take the advice of the Rev. Prebendary Stephenson, your vicar, on the matter, as he would dissuade you from such foolish notions?—Defendant: Mr. Stephenson believes it, too, but don't know what to do with her.—Thomas Cook, farmer, said he was passing complainant's cottage, when he saw the two women struggling together, and heard defendant exclaim 'I don't care now I've drawn blood from her.'—The Bench (to defendant): What does the complainant do to injure you?—Defendant: I had no rest night or day before I scratched her, and now my husband is troubled by her.—The Bench: What do you mean by hag-riding?—Defendant: A person that comes and terrifies others by night. — The Bench: Have you been troubled by her since you drew her blood?—Defendant: Not so much, but my husband is, and I'll draw it again for her if she does not leave me alone.—The Bench: We shall stop you from doing that for some time to come.—Defendant: Complainant said she wished she had a good stick for me.—The Bench: Which would have served you right.—Defendant: I have been obliged to leave Lympsham because she terrified me so.—The Bench: But what does she do to you?—Defendant: Why, I cannot stand sometimes or do anything.—The Bench: Do you see her when she terrifies you?—Defendant: Yes, I have seen her many times at night, but she does not come bodily.—The Bench: How then?—Defendant: Why, spiritually. (laughter)—The Bench: It is extraordinary to see such superstition in Lympsham. Why don't you seek the counsel of Mr. Stephenson?—Defendant: Because he believes in it as much as I do, but don't like to do anything with it.—The Bench: You are not justified in thus using Mr. Stephenson's name. It is a sad state of things to believe in such superstition, as you do, in the nineteenth century.—The Clerk: How does the complainant appear to you?—Defendant: In a nasty, evil, spiritual way, making a nasty noise.—The Bench imposed a fine of 1s. for the assault, and bound defendant over to be of good behaviour for one month, for using the threat she had in court. They also recommended defendant to consult Mr. Stephenson, who, they felt assured, would give her good advice as to her future conduct."

And more recently still, the "Daily News" of January 29th, 1875, records two other cases:—

WITCHCRAFT IN DEVONSHIRE.—"A remarkable case of credulity came before the Exeter magistrates on Wednesday. It appeared from the evidence, that a woman named Arthurs, a fortune-teller, was consulted by another woman on behalf of her son, who was suffering from some internal complaint. Arthurs pretended to read from a book the nature of the complaint and the remedy required. She also went through some mystic performances with a pack of cards, and said if the young man did not recover by a certain date he would die. Arthurs gave the woman some mixture in a bottle, for which she charged £2, but the invalid did not get better. The mother told Arthurs that she believed her son had been bewitched, and believed she was able to effect a cure. The police, however, got hold of the affair, and arrested Arthurs, who told a police officer that she had cured 'hundreds of cases,' and that 'she was very clever in that way.' A witness said she had also consulted Arthurs, and had recommended the woman in this case to her. The magistrates sent Arthurs to prison for two months, and ordered £3 found on her to be kept towards her maintenance in gaol. By a singular coincidence a witchcraft case also came before the Newton Abbott Board of Guardians on Wednesday morning. A labouring man applied for relief, saying he had been bewitched and was unable to work. In reply to the Chairman, the man said he believed in witchcraft. Admiral Wise, one of the guardians, said there was no doubt the man believed he was bewitched, and his faith could not be shaken; his illness, however, was no doubt due to a fit of appolexy. The man was granted relief, and it was suggested that the police should look after a 'wizard' who had promised to cure him."

We think the disclosures in this chapter which are by no means the worst we could make, are sufficient to show that there was a skeleton in the West, and that our efforts have not been wasted on imaginary grievances.

CHAPTER XIII.

AN ECCLESIASTICAL PHENOMENON IN THE CHURCH OF ENGLAND. A CLERGYMAN WHO RAISED HIS VOICE IN THE CAUSE OF THE OPPRESSED.*

THE REV. EDWARD GIRDLESTONE was born on September 6th, 1805; and was ordained priest in 1830. From that time till 1854 he was Vicar of Deane, in Lancashire, containing a population of 22,000, chiefly colliers and handloom weavers. It was during his long ministry in that large and laborious parish that he became familiar with, and deeply interested in, the habits and wants of the working classes. The canonry of Bristol was given him by the Crown in 1854, in recognition of services rendered to the Government in the cause of Elementary Education. It was in 1862 that he removed to Halberton, in North Devon, where the painful contrast between the miserable hovels and scant wages of the peasantry, and the good dwellings and high wages to which he had been accustomed in Lancashire, stimulated him to make some attempt to improve their condition.

His observations of the condition of the peasantry were first made in the county of Lancaster. There he

---

+ We are indebted to the "Beehive Portrait Gallery," for the particulars of the life of this truly excellent man.

had been accustomed to see the farm labourers well paid, well housed, and generally well cared for. When, therefore, in the year 1866, he took up his abode at the vicarage of Halberton, North Devon, he could not fail to be struck with the contrast presented by the miserable condition in all respects,—miserable wages, wretched hovels, and neglected state,—of the labouring class around him. When he found them receiving not more than half the remuneration given to the labourers in Lancashire, it puzzled him to understand how the unavoidable expenses incident to family life, could possibly be met out of a fund so utterly insufficient. When home and furniture of some sort had been provided, whence was food to come; if food, whence clothing; if clothing, whence schooling; whence, too, shoes, fuel, and light, to say nothing of the doctor in illness and the midwife in confinements? Perhaps, however, he said to himself, the real state of things may not be so bad as at first sight it appears. He, therefore, closely applied his mind to the investigation and consideration of the case. Having satisfied himself that the parish to which he was come might be justly regarded as a fair specimen of the whole division, he made a careful scrutiny of the facts. The weekly wages paid in money to an able bodied labourer proved to be from seven to eight shillings. To this was added a daily allowance of from three pints to two quarts of cider, of inferior quality. From this rate of payment there were two exceptions in favour of carters and of shepherds, whose hours were longer, and who therefore received a higher reward, sometimes an extra shilling a week, and in other instances a cottage and small garden rent free. In no case did the Canon meet with any other privilege than the scant one of "grist corn;" that is to say, the labourer might have from his employer, all the year round, inferior wheat at a fixed price, be the state of the market what it would. If, in dear times, this was a slight advantage, when prices fell, the farmers reaped a corresponding benefit; so that, in fact, the privilege was but nominal. Moreover, this "grist" turned out to be poor stuff, what is called "tailings," being too small in the grain to be marketable. The day's labour began at seven in the morning and ended at half-past five in the evening, with the allowance of half-an-hour for luncheon and an hour for dinner. This, however, was in name only; in point of fact, the labourers were obliged to work longer and later, sometimes from six till eight or nine, and that without any additional pay for the overtime. In harvest, when the labour was yet more protracted, they were allowed supper.

The Canon found women in the fields, and receiving seven or eight pence a day. Considering the wear and tear of clothes, this was ascertained to add little or nothing to the family fund, besides taking away mothers from their home duties. For the most part, therefore, the women worked unwillingly, and only, or chiefly, because the farmers made it a matter of bargain with the husbands that the wives should join them in their work.

Fuel, it was affirmed, was allowed to the labourer; but the explanation of the averment was, that for grubbing up the foundation of one hedge or cutting another down, after the regular day's work was done, the labourer should be permitted to carry home what he had grubbed up or cut off. As to keeping pigs or poultry, this was strictly forbidden, lest the food for fattening them should be stolen! A labourer might, indeed, have a patato patch, but only by paying to the farmer a rent four or five times the rate of that paid by the farmer to the landlord.

On what diet, then, did the labourer and his family contrive to keep body and soul together? They, or rather he, counted four meals, breakfast, forenoons (or luncheon), dinner, and supper; but of what sort? The first consisted of "tea-kettle broth;" that is, slices of bread put into a basin, over which hot water was poured, with a pinch of salt, and, on rare occasions, an onion; more rarely still, a half-teaspoonful of milk, that liquid being reserved for the farmer's pigs. The "forenoons" were nothing more than a piece of bread and a hard bit of skim-milk cheese; and dinner was no other or better. Supper was, comparatively, a feast, made up of potato and cabbage, flavoured with a little piece of bacon whenever that delicacy was available. Butcher's meat came but once a week, and for the most part less frequently than that. At an age, therefore, when husbands and fathers should be in their prime, the North Devon peasant was "crippled up" or bowed down with rheumatism, through his half-starved body remaining till night in wet clothes in that humid climate, with no fire to dry them by when at last he crawled home. In time of sickness and in premature old age, there was nothing for him but to go upon the rates; while at the best of times, there was no better home accommodation for himself and family than a wretched hovel with a slender partition in the middle, though located in a district naturally rich and boastful of its importance.

Under these circumstances the Canon's conscience would not suffer him to be a spectator of such miseries and oppressions without attempting some amelioration. In the true exercise of his sacred office, he began by trying the effect of private remonstrance. When that was set at nought, or, at any rate, was unproductive of a salutary result, he proceeded to adopt a more resolute course. It was the month of March, 1866, when the cattle plague had reached its height. Sunday had returned, and, ascending the pulpit of Halberton Church, he announced as his text, Exodus ix. 3. One may dare say, that even the stolid North Devonshire farmers pricked up their ears when they heard him enunciate the words " Behold, the hand of the Lord is upon thy cattle." But what was their consternation when the preacher plainly put it to them, whether God had not sent the murrain in token of His displeasure at their treating human labourers with less consideration than they showed to the beast of the field! But the intrepid pastor had counted the cost, and taken up a position from which all their angry indignation could not drive him. The spoken and printed abuse heaped upon him having had no deterrent effect, a plot was laid for affronting him in his own presence and in his very capacity of their lawful minister. The yearly tithe dinner was at hand; and, when the time came for drinking a toast to the Vicar's health, they would all turn their empty wine-glasses upside down and insult him to his face. But the Canon, made aware of |their intention, took care not to afford their malice an opportunity.

Meantime their contumacious deafness to his appeals left him no chance but to carry them before a wider public. In a manly letter to the *Times*, he gave a plain, clear and exact statement of the case. He was speedily overwhelmed with correspondence; not, however, taking up the farmers' quarrel. On the contrary, from other farmers residing in various parts of England, and some even of Ireland, he received numerous offers of ample work, good wages, and comfortable homes to as many of the labourers in his district as would accept them. Several persons remitted money to pay for the removal of as many men as they wanted; while, by other persons, moved by mere philanthropy, the reverend incumbent was supplied with considerable sums for his benevolent designs.* This was the origin of that system of migration from places where wages are low to places where they are comparatively high, which, wherever judiciously acted upon, has been found a source of sensible and permanent relief.

Thus backed, and misinterpreting to their own advantage the Vicar's absence when the toast to his health was to have been contumeliously declined, the farmers of Halberton mustered strong at the parish vestry, where no labourer durst appear, and refused him a church-rate for necessary purposes. Time after time they clamoured him down when he would have addressed them. He insisted nevertheless, not only upon being present at the meetings, but upon presiding in virtue of his office. As often as he opened his mouth, they did their utmost to drown his voice. In a moment of quiet, he said, 'Now, gentlemen, when you have done abusing me, we will proceed to business.' Gentlemen, forsooth! on Easter Monday, in 1867, one of them went up to the Vicar, and, in language which must not be printed, told him he was, 'unfit to carry offal to a bear. Then the whole posse claimed a right to appoint both churchwardens. This pretension was even carried up to the Court of Queen's Bench, where judgment, with costs, was given against them; and there is no point at which a Devonshire farmer feels more keenly than in his breeches pocket. This sensitiveness soon manifested itself in impotent threats of a deserted church, a breathless organ, silent bells, a voiceless choir, and forsaken schools. Nay, even Mrs. Girdlestone and her daughters were made to feel the weight of the bucolic wrath by every slight that could be put upon them. Some men would have quailed under so much malignant opposition; but the undaunted Canon was made of other stuff. Boldly and perseveringly, in the face of all, he carried out his plans with energy and method, and was rewarded with ultimate success. His migratory experiments began in the Autumn of 1866, and, by the summer of 1872, he had succeeded in sending into the Northern counties, not omitting Kent and Sussex, between four hundred and five hundred able-bodied labourers, many of them with families. In no instance was the advance of wages less than from seven shillings a week to thirteen, while in not a few instances it was as high as twenty-two, besides good cottages and gardens, both rent free.

The labour and pains which all this must have involved to Canon Girdlestone, may be imagined, but cannot here be described. The majority of the peasants were perfectly helpless. Almost everything had to be done for them; their luggage addressed, their railway tickets taken, and full and plain directions given to each by their benefactor written in a large and legible hand; many of them asking in their geographical ignorance, whether they were going "over the water." The reverend gentleman's chief, if not only, assistants in all this work of faith and labour of love, were his curate, his school-master and the members of his own family and household. But both he and they had their reward in the success which crowned their exertions, and in the lasting impulse thus given to plans for the relief of the suffering and deserving poor.

CHAPTER XIV.

The Great Arch of the Union Bridge that will Carry the Men Safe Over.

JOSEPH ARCH was born at the village of Barford in Warwickshire, in the year 1826. His father slaved and died, as most Farm Labourers do, without much hope or comfort in this world; but his mother, who thought silently over the miseries of a poor man's home, and who concluded that ignorance lay at the root of social misery, sent her son Joseph to school at the age of six, and kept him there till nine, and thus found him the key by which he succeeded in getting at some knowlege of the world beyond the bounds of the village in which he lived.

When taken from school, Joseph Arch was sent into the fields to scare birds at 4d. a day. To get something to eat himself, it was his duty to prevent the birds from eating. From this he got elevated to other kinds of agricultural work, such as ploughing, reaping, or hedging and ditching. He married early in life the daughter of a mechanic, his wages being nine shillings a week, and this was his income when there were four mouths to feed—himself, his wife, and two children—to say nothing of the poor father, whose claim on the scant meal never was denied. No word need be said in proof of the cruel poverty necessarily implied by such wages; and what was the condition of things in the home of Joseph Arch, making life a torture, was in the homes of hundreds of thousands of England's labourers doing the same powerful work. The wife of Joseph Arch, however, in a sense of womanly affection, revolted against this, and told her husband that both of them must face the world and try if, by other labour—by anything, in fact, that might turn up—such misery as they and theirs had to suffer, could be prevented. The determination was carried out by the husband, and Joseph, travelled and worked away from home, that his children might be better fed. From one thing to another Arch got on, but not by any means to affluence. He read and studied the newspapers and knew what was going on amongst the mechanics of the towns. The wrongs and the rights of labour are the same in kind all over England; they only differ in degree. Being a religious man, he became a preacher amongst the Methodists, and when a man of his class opens his mouth, if he has anything of true manhood really in him, he must soon make himself felt, not simply as a preacher in the pulpit but as an utterer of truths that touch life on its practical side, and raise questions that involve, not God's justice only, but man's justice to man in the most ordinary concerns of the world.

Fraser's Magazine of June, 1872, thus speaks of this gifted man :—

"Joseph Arch has been among the first to inaugurate a movement which is evidently destined to extend its influence over the whole country, which will probably revolutionise the life of rural England, and, in combination with the earlier organizations in the towns, in the end profoundly modify the relations of labour and capital.

Some slight signs of combination among the agricultural labourers were perceived in the winter, but seemed at first rather calculated to excite a smile than to cause either an apprehension, or a hope, that they were awakening to a consciousness that they possessed in their own hands the means of raising themselves and their offspring out of a state of dependent indigence. Weston, a small village to the north of Leamington, seems to have been the first place where an attempt at combination, for the purpose of raising wages, was made by agricultural labourers. Tidings of what had been done at Weston were brought to Wellsbourne, another village, not far from Stratford-upon-Avon; some of the labourers of this place met, and resolved to do likewise. They bethought themselves of Joseph Arch, who lived in the neighbouring village of Barford, and with whose reputation as a preacher they were well acquainted. They went to him, and asked if he would address a meeting if they could bring one together; he assented readily. We borrow from the correspondent of the *Daily News*, to whom we have already referred, his description of what followed:

'No circulars were issued calling the meeting. No advertisements appeared, nor were handbills posted. From farm to farm by word of mouth spread the tidings of a new thing in the land of stolid apathy. Over Wellsbourne Green a noble chestnut still shows its spreading arms, and under the great chestnut, on Ash Wednesday last, the agricultural labourers of South Warwickshire shook from them the fetters of centuries. Wellsbourne was present almost to a man; from the adjacent hamlets, Moreton, Locksley, Charlecote, Hampton Lucy, and other places, heavy-footed, slow-paced men converged wonderingly to the tryst under the chestnut. A thousand and more were present. Arch poured out on them his fervour: he stirred their dull intellects with the force of his reasoning. Before the meeting was done they were regenerated. Combination was urged and a union proposed.'

The men hastened eagerly to give their names to this union; other meetings were held; notices were served upon the farmers, asking for 16s. a week. These terms were refused, and thereupon the men struck work. Branches of the union formed at Wellsbourne were speedily established in many other districts in South Warwickshire. Detailed accounts of what was taking place appeared in all the newspapers, and excited a large amount of public interest and sympathy. On Good Friday a meeting of a most remarkable kind was held at Leamington, which was attended by multitudes of labourers from all the surrounding districts, accompanied in many instances by their wives. This meeting was addressed by Mr. Auberon Herbert, Joseph Arch, and others, and the foundations were laid of a union that was to comprehend all Warwickshire, and act in concert with the similar unions to be formed in the other counties of England. Already there is scarcely a county in which steps have not been taken in that direction, scarcely perhaps a parish in which the subject is not discussed, or in which men are not to be found ready to take part in this new movement.

"In this way, no doubt, Joseph Arch became an agitator, and incurred all the odium belonging to a position so detested and condemned by people who, being satisfied with things as they are, always seem in a state of alarm lest, if touched, they should be altered for the worse, so far as they are concerned. But already Joseph Arch and those who worked with him have increased the comfort in poor men's homes. More wages mean more bread; more warmth in bed on winter nights; more happiness of heart; and this is but a small part of the many blessings that must flow from the spirit of independence which agitation in the rural districts will put into the hearts of the workers in our fields. It would be hazardous to predict the full results of the movement set on foot by Joseph Arch. The falsehoods which covered the awful degradations of our rural population have been swept away like a foul fog before the freshening breeze; already the political claims of the working men in our counties have been admitted by some of our leading statesmen, and with the stout help of the workers in our towns these claims will ere long be established."

CHAPTER XV.

Rules and Constitution of the National Agricultural Labourers' Union.

JOSEPH ARCH, President.
HENRY TAYLOR, General Secretary.

Name.

1.—The National Agricultural Labourers' Union.

Object.

2.—(A.) To improve the general condition of Agricultural Labourers in the United Kingdom.

(B.)—To encourage the formation of Branch and District Unions.

(C.)—To promote co-operation and communication between Unions already in existence.

Council.

3.—A council consisting of one or more Delegates from each district Union,—the representation to be decided by the existing Executive Committee—shall meet at Leamington, or elsewhere, as may be determined by the Preceding council, on or about the third Tuesday of May, in each year, for the following purposes :—

(A.) To elect an executive Committee, together with a Treasurer, Secretary, and Trustees.

(B.) To receive a financial Statement with a Balance Sheet for the previous year, duly audited by a public accountant.

(C). To consider the General report to be submitted by Affiliated Districts for the year ending the 31st March preceding.

(D.) To confer and decide on the general business and interests of the union.

National Executive Committee.

COMPOSITION AND FUNCTIONS.

4.—The National Executive Committee shall consist of a Chairman, who shall have a second or casting vote, and of twelve Agricultural Labourers, seven of whom shall form a quorum.

5.—The National Executive Committee shall seek the counsel and co-operation of gentlemen favourable to the principles of the Union, and shall invite them to attend the meetings, without power to vote.

6.—The National Executive Committee shall meet each alternate Monday, and oftener, if necessary—all meetings to be convened by the Secretary.

7.—The National Executive Committee shall be entrusted with the expenditure of all moneys contributed by the public, by the Affiliated Districts, or otherwise; and employ the same in furthering the objects specified in Rule 2; it shall also adopt such general means as it may think desirable to carry on the work of the Union, and shall appoint paid agents and officers at discretion.

8.—The National Executive Committee shall make the necessary arrangements for each Annual Council, and shall submit a programme of the business to be considered to the Secretary of each Affiliated District at least fourteen days before the third Tuesday in May. Should any important and unforeseen circumstances arise to necessitate such a course, the National Executive Committee may at any time convoke a Special Council, upon giving the usual notice, and shall do so forthwith on the written request of six District Committees.

9.—The National Executive Committee shall communicate to the Secretary of each District Union, any proposals or suggestions that may seem advisable in the general interests of the Union as a whole.

Settlement of Disputes.

10.—All classes of dispute between the Members of the National Agricultural Union and their Employers must be laid before the Branch Committee to which such Members belong; and should the Branch Committee be unable to arrange the question to the mutual satisfaction of the parties interested, in conjunction with the District Committee, recourse shall be had to arbitration. Should the District Committee, be unable to arrange for such arbitration, an appeal shall be made to the National Executive Committee for its decision. Any award made by arbitration or by decision of the National Executive, shall be binding upon all Members of the Union; and in no case shall a strike be resorted to, until the above means have been tried and failed.

11.—That at no time shall the privilege of reduction in hours and rise of wages, be demanded at one time.

12.—The National Executive Committee shall determine anything wherein the Society's rules are silent; but in no case shall they alter the established rules of the Society.

Financial.

13.—The funds of the National Agricultural Labourers' Union shall be invested in the names of the following gentlemen as Trustees:—Mr. A. Arnold, Hampton-in-Arden; Mr. Jesse Collings, Birmingham; Mr. E. Jenkins, London.

14.—The Treasurer shall make no disbursements except on receipt of a resolution of the National Executive Committee, signed by the Chairman and Secretary; at the first Meeting in each month he shall present a Cash Statement to the National Executive, and shall deposit, at interest, in the names of the Trustees, with Lloyd's Bank at Leamington, any sum in his hands exceeding £500.

District Committees.

15.—District Committees shall bear the name of the County or division embracing them, as the "Kent District," or the "West Berks District of the National Agricultural Labourers' Union." District Committees shall be composed of Delegates from the various branches of the District; and each District Committee shall elect an Executive of seven Members, together with a Chairman, Secretary, and Treasurer, who shall meet monthly and oftener when necessary.

16.—Each District Committee shall regulate its own affairs in conformity with the general principles laid down in the preceding Rules; but no Rules drawn up by any Branch shall be accepted by the National Agricultural Labourers' Union unless they shall first have been ratified by the District Committee to which such Branch belongs.

17.—District Committees shall do their utmost to prevent men who may migrate to another locality from underbidding their fellow Labourers already at work there.

18.—Each District Committee shall be required at its own cost to send a Delegate or Delegates to the Meetings of the Council.

19.—Each District Committee shall send to the National Executive Committee, on or before the fourteenth of every month, a brief Report of its proceedings; and on the third Friday in April, July, October, and January, under a penalty of 10s. for neglect, a Financial Statement, with the balance due on the quarter.

20.—Each District Committee must inform the National Executive Committee of any important action contemplated within its jurisdiction; and, should any proceedings be taken by a district without the sanction of the National Executive Committee and be persisted in after the National Executive has signified its disapproval, such District shall not be assisted in its action by the funds of the National Agricultural Labourers' Union.

21.—That each District issue a Balance Sheet, audited and printed, at the end of each financial quarter, and supply one to each Branch in the District; also the Secretary of each District shall supply one to each other affiliated District; as early as possible.

22.—All districts wishing to be affiliated with the National Agricultural Labourers' Union must remit three-fourths of the entrance fees and of the weekly contributions to the National Executive Committee, to be invested and employed in accordance with previous rules.

23.—Cards of Membership bearing the device of the National Agricultural Labourers' Union, shall be issued to the district Committees, to be supplied by them to their several Branches. The contribution cards to be double.

Branches.

24.—Each Branch shall bear the name of the village or parish in which its business is transacted.

25.—Branches shall consist of farm and other Labourers, of one or more parishes in the same locality, who shall pay an entrance fee of 6d., and a weekly contribution of $2\frac{1}{4}$d., the farthing to be appropriated to the management expenses of the Branch.

26.—Branches, as soon as practicable, shall unite in forming themselves into Districts.

27.—Each Branch shall annually elect a chairman, Treasurer, Secretary, and a Committee of seven Members, for the Management of its business, to communicate with the District Executive, and through it with the National Executive.

28.—Branches shall meet fortnightly for the payment

of contributions and other business.

29.—The Chairman shall preside at each meeting of the Branch; he shall preserve order, promote the interests and repute of the Union to the best of his power, and sign all reports, minutes, etc. The Secretary shall keep the accounts of the Branch, record the minutes of all the Meetings, and pay over all funds to the Treasurer without loss of time. The Treasurer shall receive all monies, and under a penalty of 2s. for neglect, shall, in conjunction with the Secretary, remit them to the District Executive on the first Thursday in every month, together with an audited account.

30.—Branches shall be at liberty to frame any bye-laws they may think necessary—regard being had Rule 16.

31.—These Rules shall be subject to additions or alteration only by the Annual or a special Council. One month's notice of any intended Amendment must be given to the Secretary in writing, and such amendment shall not be adopted unless two-thirds of the Delegates present approve it by vote.

CHAPTER XVI.

Autobiography and Recollections of "One from the Plough."

I am told by people, who ought to know, that I was born at Montacute, near Yeovil, in the County of

Somerset, on the Sixth day of February, 1827. I know of my own knowlege that I was "growed" in the aforesaid village, and "dragged up" pretty hard. My parents were very poor. My father had worked long enough upon a farm to learn the cider.—Yes, he learned that lesson too well—he got a love of cider into his disposition, which unfortunately kept him poorer than he otherwise might have been, for he had the good sense to quit farm labouring when a young man, but as he became a stone-mason on Ham Hill in the immediate neighbourhood, he merely took refuge in the Frying-pan,* in order to be out of the fire, the rate of pay on the Hill being then, as now, kept down to the lowest figure by the depressing influence of the starvation wages paid to agricultural labourers all around.

Although my father earned 12/- a week at the quarries, nearly double the wages of a farm labourer at that time, I was brought up in the greatest poverty and misery, just about on a par with the wretched ploughmen's families in the village.

I had to go to work at 5 years old for sixpence per week with scarce any clothes, only what my mother could beg from other people for me. I was sent at this early age to keep away rooks from the seed corn.

---

* The Frying-pan of Ham Hill is an old Roman Circus. The stone from this hill, known as Ham Stone is of great beauty and durability. It is especially suitable for churches and other public buildings. In my opinion it is the handsomest, as well as the best stone to stand the weather, in this country. Had the Houses of Parliament and Buckingham Palace been built of this stone they would not have been so troublesome to their architects. The Marquis of Salisbury did one sensible thing in his life when he introduced Ham Stone into the Green Park.

The whole family were obliged to make the utmost exertions to get food to eat. We never tasted meat except an "accident" happened among the sheep or cattle, or one of the flocks and herds was down with consumption or the "gunn," a sort of leprosy, then the farmer would have one killed *to save its life* when we could be indulged with a little diseased meat at 3d. or 4d. a pound.

I had to trudge about the fields from dawn to dark in all weathers, going to my work in summer as early as 4 o'clock in the morning with nothing but a morsel of bread for my breakfast. I had also to work on Sundays. I was always glad when the snow came, for then I was able to go home for a little while. I was often wet through from 5 o'clock in the morning till night, when my wet clothes formed the principal part of my bed covering, while the heat of my body dried them for the next day, for there was often no fire to dry them by.

Our food consisted principally of a little barley-cake, potatoes and salt, tea kettle broth, and barley "flippet." Tea kettle broth consists of a few pieces of bread soaked in hot water with a little salt, sometimes with a leek chopped up in it. Never do I remember a sufficient quantity of bread being used for the spoon to stand upright in. Barley flippet was made by sprinkling barley-meal into a pot of boiling water, which, when sufficiently thickened, was served up with salt and sometimes a little treacle.

Now and then I got what we used to call a hot dinner, that is to say, a piece of bread and an onion, at others, a bit of bread and hard skim-cheese—so hard that I had to soak it in water before I could eat it. This cheese would have made capital foundations for a house.

But had we enough even of this kind of food? No, indeed! I was frequently sent off to work with the promise of a breakfast, as there was no bread in the house, but in wet weather, or when, as often was the case they had no food at home, I had to go without. When I got home at night, I many times found my father and mother so irritable from privation, that they would send me to bed without my supper as a pretended punishment, when, in reality, they had no food for me.

Sometimes I would pull a turnip in the fields and gnaw it to prevent hunger gnawing me. If I could find peas, beans or acorns, I would eat as many as I could get, and many a time have I hunted and foraged about for snails in the hedges and roasted them for my lunch or tea. This was a common occurrence. Of a night after leaving off these festivities, when I went to the farm house, I was occasionally sent on an errand miles away without any supper, for which I received no payment, but a cup of vinegar water, commonly called cider, but utterly unfit for any human being to drink. It was called by the men, "pummy's wash."

The process of cider-making is as follows:—They take the apples and mix them in judicious proportions, sweet and sour together, and put them into a mill where they grind them into a coarse kind of pulp which is placed in layers, upon neatly arranged straws, under a powerful press and the screw is applied by two or three strong men who make the pulp into a very compact "cheese" as it is called.

The juice having thus been run off, has merely to be placed in tubs to ferment, and after racking into casks, is fit for drinking.

But do the farm labourers get this delightful, natural and healthful drink? Oh, no! The old casks are washed out with water which is carefully preserved along with the washings of the cider press and all other utensils connected with the manufacture, and the "cheese" is broken up and digested in these washings and then pressed again, while in order to set up alcoholic fermentation, they take the skum and froth from the top of the genuine fermenting juice and add it to this dirty water, which thus becomes half an intoxicating drink and half vinegar, that easily intoxicates starving men, while it eats into the bones of poor skeletons without any fatty or glutinous matter about them to sheath their poor frames, half composed of lime, from the action of this acid.

I continued year after year in this wretched slavery subject to the greatest harshness and cruelty. My master used to thrash me unmercifully whenever he was offended with himself or anyone else or nothing at all. Sometimes I remonstrated with him as the burning tears of shame and pain and sense of wrong fell upon my rough smock— I asked him why he beat me, and what for? As he could not tell why I deserved it, I suppose he gave it me by the time I did.

The savage cruelty and brutality of the farmers, and of course, the men also, which I have seen practised towards poor little boys and girls who were sent out to work in the fields entirely beggars all description. It often makes my blood boil and curdle and tingle now. I cannot bear to think of it—I would forget if I could. I have seen great girls exposed in the most shameful manner before men and boys and beaten till the blood came, merely for the brutal pastime or at the malicious caprice of the farmer. I have known stewards and shepherds cut the strongest and toughest ash and hazel sticks out of the hedge, to lay about them on the tender backs of boys scarcely grown out of infancy. If one such case of cruelty to children came before a London magistrate, the greatest public indignation would be expressed and the offender would be severely punished, while in the country, parents know it is of no use to appeal to justice, for parsons and landlords always side with the farmers, who order their gangers to carry on this cruelty as a system of slave-driving, and the more cruel these men are, the better they get on.

As to the ordinary rank and file labourer, he often got beaten himself in the the bad old times,—not old enough to be times of plenty and independence, times of monasteries and common-lands, and not recent enough to be times of Labourers' Unions, and School Boards. I can bring irrefutable evidence to prove that quiet, respectful, hard-working men were beaten by the farmers, especially married men with long families who were dependent upon their masters for their miserable homes.

One Summer Sunday morning when I was with the sheep, changing them from field to field, I was singing and whistling merrily, forgetting all my youthful sufferings, when my master (this was at Windmill Farm) came up with a ground ash stick and thrashed me across my arms and back until he was obliged to leave off from the violence of the exertion. I cried to him "Maister, what d'ye do that for? I 'ant done nothing wrong." I repeatedly begged him to tell me what was the reason for this barbarous treatment—on a Sunday, too, when I knew I was working for no pay and ought to have been at Sunday School. He had no answer for me. He slunk away like a man who had come with a murderous intent, had done his foul work, and his thirst for blood was sated.

I then ran away home with the blood trickling down my shirt, and never went back to that merciless villain any more. My father and mother dared not interfere. The magistrates always sided with the farmers, and it was well-known to be worse than useless to hope for any justice whatever from parsons and squires.

I, however, was sent to Abbey Farm, where I got little better treatment. I had a small advance of wages, but much harder work. I continued at this farm until I was 19 years of age. When I could hold my own plough and drive my own horses, I only had 1/10 a week, and often ploughed as much in a day as a man.

It would be impossible to relate all the sufferings and privations I endured and witnessed during my boyhood, and I sometimes think what my fate would have been if I had remained at the plough all my life. The men who were ploughboys with me have chiefly died out, but those who are left, are infirm old men, though not yet fifty, quite disabled, given over, as S.G.O. well-said, to pauperism and rheumatism.

CHAPTER XVII.

A Glance at my Native Village, and How I came to Leave it.

THE Village of Montacute is quite a place by itself. There is nothing like it anywhere else. It once contained the second monastery in the kingdom, and the old-fashioned narrow street hugs a fine gothic church tower and the remains of an abbey, once united as a vast house of charity, intended, no doubt, for the benefit of the poor, and was unquestionably public property. The tendency of aristocratic legislation, however, has always been and is now, to take away the property of the poor and give it to the rich, and that's what was done with Montacute Abbey. It is now a picturesque farm house under the shade of Michael's Mount or Miles Hill or Mice Hill as it is variously called, and is still ornamental if no longer useful to the public.

This Miles Hill is a peculiar feature of my native village. It is a sugar-loaf mound covered with trees, and, no doubt this *mont acute*, as it was called by the Norman emigrants, gave my old local habitation, a name.

But the whole neighbourhood abounds in objects of great beauty, and a visit to Montacute would delight every lover of truly rural scenery. They must take smelling bottles with them though, for the sanitary arrangements of the village are abominable. Most of the houses have no garden whatever, are crowded together as though land was worth ten thousand pounds an acre. Many of the cottages are unfit for human habitation and epidemic diseases are frequent visitors.

As however is the case with most English villages, there is one house, the size and splendour of which contrasts notably with the squalor of the other dwellings. This, of course, is the temple of that local god, the squire. The mansion of the Phelips family is one of the finest in the county. It was built by Inigo Jones, in Elizabethan Gothic, with handsome groups of spiral chimneys and statuary. It contains a chamber over 200 feet in length, and the height of the house is nearly 100 feet. As a public building it would be an ornament and a pride to any place, but I am not proud of so much space and dwelling-room being monopolised by one person, especially when such mansions do not pay their quota of taxation.

I may as well point out here that the richest people pay the least taxes upon their property. The house taxes paid by the following noblemen, are as follows:—

	PER ANNUM.		
	£	s.	d.
The Duke of Bedford, for Woburn Abbey	26	8	0
The Duke of Devonshire, for Chatsworth	56	3	0
The Duke of Marlborough, for Blenheim Palace	16	7	6
The Marquis of Salisbury, for Hatfield House	33	15	0

Now, I don't suppose I shall be far wrong if I place

Montacute House in the list of under-taxed palaces, and probably the reason why the poor are so crowded is because the small houses are over-taxed to make up the deficiency in the impost on great ones. Henry Brouncker, Esq., a celebrated New Forest Conservative has given important evidence upon this point, and there is scarcely a parish in the kingdom where this injustice is not done. This is known and deplored by the farmers, but they dare not interfere.

My old master protested against the under-rating of Montacute House, and he soon had to leave Abbey Farm. I do not say that he received notice in consequence of this protest, I only mention two facts and leave my readers to draw their inferences.

Then the Squire of Montacute is an absentee landlord. He draws all his revenue from that district and spends it somewhere else. I don't think William the Conqueror would have allowed that. This may add to the poverty of my old fellow villagers, and may be one reason why the farm labourers of Montacute are almost an extinct race. Montacute House has not been regularly inhabited for forty years, and yet during that period nearly half a million of money has been extracted from this poverty-stricken district by one man, to be spent Heaven knows where and Goodness knows how. It is said that "Property has its duties as well as its rights" but the Montacute property has more than its rights, while its duties are lost sight of altogether.

For instance, during that period, the people have been deprived of their right to two fat oxen every Christmas, which were to be given in perpetuity in exchange for common-lands enclosed, so that the poor "Munticue volk" as they are called in the Somersetshire brogue, are owed eighty fat oxen now.

Again, in the old squire's time (he *was* a fine old English gentleman, and no mistake), the people had some of the very best land for allotment gardens at a very low price, but a few years ago they were turned out of the grounds they had manured and improved, and were given exhausted corn lands instead, at a rental of three times its value. It was cruel to see the enormous crops the farmer reaped from these poor people's gardens which he had taken as a field.

The potato famine was a sad visitation for Montacute. The people had hitherto been as dependent upon potatoes as were the Irish themselves, and the poor of the village suffered bitterly without any helping hand being extended to them. No money was collected for *their* relief. I don't know what the lords and gentry, the bishops and parsons were about then, but certainly they were not equal to the occasion. I believe one nobleman gave the poor his advice at the time, which was to use curry powder. That was something like the French Queen, who, when she heard that her subjects had no bread to eat, exclaimed, "Why don't they eat cake then?"

This potato famine, of course, made corn very dear, yet wheat was kept back to be eaten by rats in order to make it still dearer, and indeed it is said that large quantities were thrown into the water to prevent its coming into the market, so that the food of the people should rise to a forced price; and more men, women and children were starved to death at that time than died natural deaths—Aye, and I further say, that a coroner's inquest ought to be held over many a dead farm labourer now, and a verdict of "wilful murder" returned against "some person or persons." "A skeleton at the plough!" Why, I was for years at the plough without any proper food whatever, a growing lad, with hunger gnawing my vitals; and can I now forget the poor plough-boys whose condition is very nearly as bad as mine was? Can I bid the men be content under a system of injustice and wrong both in church and state, which has caused all this?

No towns-people have any idea of the poverty of such places as Montacute at the time I speak of, and Goodness knows it's bad enough now. I ask any lady or gentleman to imagine such "tea" as we were forced to put up with. A piece of black crust of bread put in the kettle and sweetened with treacle! And often we had nothing but a few boiled swede turnips for our suppers—sometimes a feast of turnip-greens, or turnip-tops, as they are generally called, and sometimes nothing at all. Boys must be well-nigh starving to eat snails, acorns and hawthorn-berries, and go down on their knees to drink the butter-milk out of the pig's trough, and bare their arms to dive into it for morsels of curd and other delicacies "that the swine did eat."

However, at nineteen, I found myself, after rises of 3d. and 6d. earning exactly 4/- per week, and I was certainly very discontented with my lot. I wanted to learn the stone work, but my father, though he had become a master mason, objected to my leaving the farm, since it was so convenient for my mother to get grist corn, cider, skim-cheese and other things on a sort of truck system, on the strength of my miserable wages, and he would not teach me the trade of a mason.

One day I had risen as usual at 4 o'clock, harrowed a field of turnip seed on Butcher's Hill, and then went hay-carrying. I loaded for two pitchers from noon till night, that is to say, I so disposed the hay upon the waggon that it formed a firm and consistent load. After 18 hours hard work without two-penn'orth of victuals in my stomach, only a few cold potatoes, it being now night, I felt quite exhausted, having had no real nourishment and lay down on a poke of hay. This was in a field called Doctor's Whitcomb. My master ordered me to unload the last waggon, which was not my regular duty. I replied that I could do no more. He then began to swear and call me bad names, one of which was "lazy young dog," or something worse, and he attempted to kick me as I lay. Just then I heard Montacute clock strike 10, so I bade him a very good night, and went home tired as a dog, but very much hurt in my mind that I had been called the lazy son of one. I trudged home, down Hollow Lane, resolving to bear that kind of life no more, and as I groped in the dark for my supper, a few more cold "taters," I inly swore that I would take leave of Montacute as soon as possible. Next day (Thursday) was pay-day, and I gave my master a fortnight's notice to leave. My master was surprised and asked me where I was going. I said, I meant to go masoning on Ham Hill. He asked, why? I replied, because fourteen shillings a week was better than seven. He said, I was now too old to learn a trade and that I should never earn 14/- a week in this world. I said, I would try. Within eighteen months from that time I received 17/9 per week, and caused a letter to be written home to tell my master that he could now fill my place, as I had so far exceeded the 14/-

The people about the farm were alarmed at my presumption and thought I should come to grief. They therefore remonstrated with me and begged and prayed of me not to be rash but to remain where I was.

At the expiration of the fortnight the farmer gave me two shillings in addition to my wages, saying, that I had worked very hard and was entitled to another shilling. I said, I ought to have seven shillings as I did a man's work. He replied, "So you shall when you get married," for that is the rule, to give an extra two shillings a week as premium on early marriages, that the farmer may get the woman's services in haying and harvest, and the children's work for the merest trifle. I asked him if he thought 2/- a week was enough to keep a wife? His answer was, "That's no business of mine," I said, "Then its my business, and I'll spend this two shillings in shoeleather to carry me away from a place where five shillings is considered enough to keep a young man and two shillings sufficient to maintain a young woman." He exclaimed, " Ah, George, thee'st be glad enough to come back again in a month!" But that month has been a long one.

Well, in spite of my father's objection to teach me his trade, I went to Ham Hill and learnt stone-sawing, but could not at first get on as a mason, the drinking customs of the quarry were so hindering to anything like prosperity and progress, that one Saturday I resolved to leave the neighbourhood altogether.

CHAPTER XVIII.

A Pilgrimage from Poverty to Competence.

ON the Monday following I started off on foot in the direction of Bath, with a few half-pence I had saved, being chiefly the proceeds of playing the flute in a band. I had no notion where I was going any more than that I knew there was a deal of stonework at Bath. I called in at the village of Doulton, near Shepton Mallet, where I got a job. There I worked for some time and managed to save £3 or £4. My employer kept back a week's money because I should not go away, and the last week's wages are owing to me still, for I wanted to improve myself and determined to go back to Ham Hill to learn the business of a mason thoroughly. I had seen the architectural drawings on the hill and the masons planning out gothic windows, and carved work, and I desired to reach the highest position as a skilled workman in that trade. I worked there for some time and got a better insight into practical masonry. I then went with a Ham

Hill man to Wells, and being disappointed in obtaining work there, went on to Chewton Mendip where they were building water-works for Bristol. I became employed on these water-works at Chewton Mendip, but did not stay there long on account of the miserable and indecent state of the lodgings. During a part of that summer I slept in a stall rather than crowd with men, women and children in one room, especially with people who believed in witchcraft, and were utterly ignorant of the most common things, and had no more idea of propriety or decency than the ox in the stall.

I next made for Bath, that paradise of stonemasonry, but was quite unsuccessful there, and hearing that a church was building at Norton St. Philip's, I proceded thither, and was fortunate in finding a kind master, which was something new to me. I am bound to say that the builder, Mr. Brown, of Frome, was the best friend I ever had in early life. He was a gentleman all over, and my meeting with him was a turning point of my life. My money was nearly all spent when I reached there, and the man who was with me was a hindrance to me rather than a help. I had to plead hard to get him a job also. I saved money there.

I next went to Kingston Deverell, where there was a church being built on the Marquis of Bath's estate. Lodgings were difficult to obtain to suit a decent working man, so I was obliged to get house-room where I could. I found a farm labourer's cottage where they took lodgers, but was surprised to find that a father, mother, grown up daughters, sons and lodgers, ten persons in all, slept in one room. I felt very much ashamed of it but could get no other accommodation. I was bound to have that or nothing. There were no conveniences whatever, to carry out the ordinary and proper decencies of life. I much regret that I am unable to relate the scenes I witnessed in that lodging. The whole story ought to be told, but if I had not too much respect for the general reading public to suppress the shameful details, I am sure that my printer would have more respect for himself than to put them into type.

This low state of social life in a village, which to casual passers through the place would appear to be a paradise of rural beauty, innocence and virtue, is but a sample of Somersetshire villages, and was quite explained by the scenes enacted at the opening of the church.

When this event took place, instead of behaving like christians, the people made a fair of it, carrying on the most brutal and blackguardly sports during the day, and the lowest of drunken revelry at night. The clergy of the Church of England are responsible for this state of things. Instead of endeavouring to raise the condition of their people, it is, unfortunately, their interest to keep them down to the lowest level, in order that their patrons may get the utmost out of the farmers, and this state of things will never be altered until the church is disestablished, and is entirely free from state control, nor shall we have a higher tone of morality until we have men chosen by the people and not by the landlords.

After this, I revisited my native place, and finding a relative contemplating a journey to London, I agreed to keep him company, and have had no cause to regret the step I so willingly took.

As I was always a frugal and temperate liver, I invariably saved money when I was in work, so that, although I had been down to Montacute for a holiday and had not been sparing of my cash, I had enough left to maintain me in London for some time in case of being unsuccessful in finding employment.

A good many working men have said they would like to take a leaf out of my book, and have been very curious to know the method by which I have attained my commercial status in London; and I have long promised many friends to give a full, true and particular account of myself, in order that they may go and do likewise if they please.

Now, there is no magic about it. I found no Aladdin's Lamp, I discovered no gold mine—I had no revelation from above or below how to make money. My road to competence was the straight and narrow way of enterprise and determination in migrating from depressed and crowded districts in quest of the best work to be had, then in giving plenty of good work for my money and so gaining the confidence of my employers, then in spending less than half my earnings. My life of extreme poverty had so accustomed me to privation that I could live well, as I then considered it, on 7/- or 8/- a week. I remained single. I did not drag the girl I loved into matrimony and misery, so that I had only myself to keep, and began life with no burdens. *I did not drink*—that is to say, I did not make a practice of spending my earnings in beer and spirits; I attended church or chapel regularly, and so gained rest in body and mind, to gather up my energies for the next week's work.

Finding, as I thought, more homeliness and spirituality among the dissenters, I soon joined the Wesleyan body, since they invited me to do so (rather a shy young man with a strong sense of my own awkwardness) and the Baptists did not, or I think I had a leaning towards their peculiar doctrines.

The Methodists now induced me to become a Sunday School teacher, and in a moment of weakness I consented to do so, although at this time I could scarcely read, and had never learnt to make a pot-hook. Why was this? Simply because the clergy and gentry of my neighbourhood intended that I should be a slave all my days, and denied me the greatest happiness of life, KNOWLEDGE.

Well, I took a class of very little children, as I *had* learnt my ABC at the Baptist Sunday School, Montacute, where I remained but a short time, as farm labour kept me at work on Sundays, and I had, therefore, but few opportunities to learn anything. I was now utterly ashamed to find that these infant Wesleyans were far ahead of me in their reading and that I could rather learn of them than teach them anything. I may say that I learnt to read by teaching it. However, I was for twenty-three years a Sunday School Teacher, and if I was five minutes behind, the children thought some accident had happened.

I fortunately had a master who employed me winter and summer, because he appreciated my exertions and did not wish to lose me. As I was saving a pound every week and sometimes more, I determined to learn to write, for which purpose I walked from Battersea to Covent Garden and back every evening, until I had so far accomplished my object, that I could write my own love-letters, and as I have since found, make out my own estimates, bills and cheques, and otherwise conduct a large business.

While I was working for a stone and marble mason, my department was the rougher occupation of stone masonry, and as I spoke the "Zummerzetsheer" brogue, the other men used to laugh and chaff, and call me the "soft stone" mason. One day I ventured to tell a marble mason, that I could work his material as well as my own, at which he contemptuously defied me ever to learn the marble work, and said that it was not in me. I quietly waited till he was away at dinner, when I took up his tools and performed a quantity of his work in precisely the same manner as he did it himself, but when he found me thus employed he was very angry and called our employer to see how I had spoiled his work. The master said he could not see it. Then the man said either he or I should go, and the result was, that I took up his task which he had excited me to try my hand on, and completed it.

At the time of the Exhibition of 1851, I was asked by an architect and a builder, to take a contract for some stone and marble work, but they wanted a guarantee. My last master had just died, so I had to apply to an old employer to do this favour for me. He very handsomely went up and said he would guarantee me for £2,000, and, in fact, he so satisfied them, that no more was said about any guarantee whatever.

I got on by degrees, not spending my money at pot-houses or among loose characters, but saving it for future undertakings. I employed and enjoyed my Sabbaths at the chapel and the Sunday school. When the secession from the great Wesleyan body took place, I joined the followers of Dunn and Everett, always sympathising with the cause of progress and freedom, whether in Church or State. I have the greatest respect for the old Wesleyan body, but wealth and power *will* make the best of churches blindly tyrannical. The Conference made a mistake. The ministers of a voluntary church, attempted to coerce the brethren who differed from them. They endeavoured to quash a free press in their midst, and this was fatal to the unity of Methodism. The great schism, as churchmen would call it and as Wesleyans *have* called it, of the United Free Methodist Church, became an accomplished fact, and I am proud to say that I have filled every office in that church, except preacher, which a man could occupy. I have been mostly associated with members of the more recent organization, but I have found that men of business who rejoice in the name of Methodist, so far as I have had dealings with them, are men of the strictest integrity and uprightness.

My course was now rather more smooth, as I had the fore-horse by the head and became the employer of labour. I was fortunate in making some money by contracts, and in seven years after my arrival in London, found myself worth nearly £3000.

CHAPTER XIX.

AUTOBIOGRAPHY CONCLUDED. A REVERSE, REVERSED. HOW I CAME TO TAKE UP THE CAUSE OF THE AGRICULTURAL LABOURERS.

NOT having been brought up to commercial pursuits, I was not so careful as I ought to have been, as to who I trusted. I believed everyone honest, and allowed myself to be drawn in too deep in one direction. My eggs were all in one basket. One man owed me all I was worth. He was temporarily unfortunate in a building speculation, and failed. In one day all my savings were gone and I found myself with a wife and two children, penniless! If I had yielded to the advice of kind friends, who bade me pay *them*, sell up and offer my creditors a composition, I should have been again thrown back upon a dependent position, but I preferred to take the bull by the horns:—I went straight up to my principal creditors and told them my position. Bad news travels fast. They knew of my misfortune and were ready to help me. I said to one, "If my next bill should be returned to you, will you wait a little while?" And the reply was, "Go on just as before. We shall not ask you for any money, until you have turned yourself round." Another actually offered to lend me whatever I required. But I would not borrow. All I wanted was time, in case it was required, but as it turned out I got in sufficient to take up every bill, and but few persons knew that anything had been the matter.

The chief annoyance I experienced was through the importunities of my "*friends*," to whom I was indebted in any way, and also their bewailings and reproofs, their bitter sympathy and bilious pity. Well, they never had to wait a day over their time for payment, nor had any of my work people to go short for one hour. My reverse was soon reversed. The building trade supported me manfully—in the course of time a better dividend came in than I expected, and in two or three years I was stronger than ever.

After this, I continued to prosper for many years, as in spite of much enmity I still do, until I have accumulated the finest stock of its kind in Europe. It is my practice to keep on the best workmen I can get, whether I have orders for their work or not, so that in slack times their work accumulates, and as I am constantly importing foreign work in anticipation of special orders, my collection of marble has grown to be such, that nothing but personal inspection can give a just idea of its variety and extent.

I must now briefly allude to the circumstances which led to my advocacy of the National Agricultural Labourers' Union. When I left the plough I solemnly promised my old field-mates that if prosperity attended my steps, I would do everything in my power to help them out of their poverty, and for many years I carried on a system of migration among the Montacute labourers. I employed and still employ many of these men. I went backwards and forwards to my native village encouraging migration and emigration. I became a correspondent to the local press, and wrote many letters of protest against the shameful system of slavery under which so large a body of Englishmen and Englishwomen were suffering, and I published the following Balance Sheet which created a great stir among the farmers:—

A Devon and Somerset Agricultural Labourers' Balance Sheet.

From Pulman's Weekly News, Crewkerne.

The following is an Account of a Year's Earnings and Expenditure of John————, an Agricultural Labourer not a hundred miles from Axminster and Yeovil, in full employment. His case is not the miserable lot of one, but of many thousands of his class, who are in as bad and still worse situation. John received from his employer, between Lady-Day, 1871, and Lady-Day 1872, £19 16 6 for Piece-work (Hedging, Draining, Turnip-hoeing, Mowing and Harvesting) and £12 for Day-work at 10s. a week, inclusive of Twenty-one Days Lost Time on account of Bad Weather. Thus, this fine young English Labourer's total year's income was £31 16 6, besides three pints of Cider on six days of the week, and none on Sundays.

"Let us now turn to the debit side of the account, and the items shall be furnished by John's wife, a careful and notable woman. For you must understand that John has a wife and four children to provide for out of his earnings:

	£	s.	d.
Rent 2s. a week	5	4	0
Poor Rates	0	7	6
Tithes	0	1	6
One cwt. of Coals a week	2	12	0
One Year's Shoes for each of the family, and mending a year	2	5	0
Bread, 4s. 6d. per week	14	14	0
Quarter-Acre of Potato Ground	2	0	0
Seed Potatoes	1	0	0
Club pay	0	12	0
Half a lb. of Soap a week	0	10	10
Tea, 3d. a week	0	13	0
Candles, 20 weeks	0	7	6
Quarter lb. of Butter week	0	17	4
Half a lb. of Treacle a week	0	6	6
Matches, Thread and Tape	0	3	6
Broom and Salt	0	2	0
Two Cups and Saucers	0	0	4
Four Plates and Four Mugs	0	1	4
Four Children's Schooling, at 1d. a week	0	17	4
Tools—Scythe, Two Hooks, Whetstones, Pickaxe, Gloves, Two Shovels, Cross-axe, Spade, Turnip Hoe	1	12	10
Repairing ditto	0	5	3
Total	31	13	9

Leaving a Balance of 2/9 to buy the family Butcher's

Meat, Clothing and other absolute necessaries, for which. if procured at all, the Village Shopkeeper and the Travelling Packman must be the sufferers.

John is in hope of being better off, for his master (a guardian) has promised to get him a shilling or two a week from the Union. But he says he must first see the doctor, and get some of his family upon the Sick List.

P.S.—It is a well-known fact that three-fourths of the Farm Labourers of Devon and Somerset are only receiving Eight Shillings per week, and some with 14 children, therefore Meat and Clothes are entirely out of the Question.

(Signed) **ONE FROM THE PLOUGH**

I felt, after all, that I was powerless to affect the great mass of injustice and degradation, so that when I heard of the movement in Warwickshire, I soon became convinced that the whole of the West of England must be united to that organization in order to accomplish any general reform.

At first, I laboured under a prejudice against trades' unions, a prejudice, no doubt, fostered by persons interested in keeping the working class party as weak as possible.—Still I had imbibed the poison, and I was somewhat doubtful whether the trades' union leaders and "agitators" were not so many personifications of the Evil One. I was, however, gratefully surprised to find, that they had neither horns, hoofs, nor tails, and as to the N.A.L.U. delegates,

I found them to be mostly Methodist local preachers and teetotalers.

I may here mention that other organizations are doing good work for the Agricultural Labourers, notably the Federal, but I wish there could be an amalgamation of the whole forces in order to fight the men's battle against tyranny, fraud and cruelty, and furthermore, I am bound to say, that a spirit of division and opposition will never be encouraged by disinterested men, while if personal interests were not allowed to keep apart those two great bodies, both working for the same ends, a truly "national" union might be amalgamated, which could include the majority of the million farm labourers of the country, and become a vast power for good in every conceivable way.

Already, this movement has become politically important. Nearly a million of hard-working men have newly learnt the principles of combination, the value of education and the necessity of political power in order that their wants shall be respected. And that these long neglected serfs will soon have the suffrage extended to them I confidently hope and believe.

CHAPTER XX.

A MEETING AT MY NATIVE VILLAGE, AND THE FORMATION OF A BRANCH.

The following is from Pulman's Weekly Newspaper June 4th, 1872.

WEEKLY NEWS OFFICE, TUESDAY MORNING.

THE AGRICULTURAL LABOUR QUESTION.

GREAT MEETING AT MONTACUTE LAST (MONDAY) EVENING.

FOR some days past the Village of Montacute has been placarded with bills drawing attention to "the low wages of the labourers," and last week a bill was circulated intimating that a meeting was to be held yesterday (Monday) evening, when Mr. G. Potter, Mr. G. Mitchell and several other gentlemen would deliver addresses. Of course this caused considerable excitement. The prime mover seems to be Mr. George Mitchell, marble mason, of London, formerly a labourer at Montacute, but who has been fortunate in business. Knowing the wages at Montacute, he expressed himself anxious that the labourers should take advantage of the prevailing excitement to get an increase. He accordingly induced delegates from London and Leamington to attend.

Towards the hour fixed for the meeting, men walked into the village from all directions, and considerable interest appeared to be taken in the proceedings. A platform was erected in the Square, which was taken possession of by the fife and drum band. The audience was principally composed of working men, who were exceedingly orderly throughout and patiently listened to every speaker. The number present, including the wives of the men, could not be less than 1,500.

Mr. George Mitchell was received with cheers. Their object in coming there was not, as it had been asserted, to spread strife or to sow the seeds of discord. A person had charged him with causing strife, but he had written a letter to him in reply, and he had had no intimation that it would be answered. Montacute men were as good as Yorkshiremen, and as honest as any class in the country. He had been introduced to them as one from the plough, and if anyone would stand up and say that he was not from the plough he would challenge, at the end of a month, to plough any farmer in Montacute for £50, the winner to give the amount to the poor of Montacute. (Cheers.) He saw in front of him several companions with whom he used to plough, although he wished that they had a little more "grub." (Laughter.) A few potatoes and a drop of bacon fat once in a day was not sufficient for any man. (Laughter, cheers, and voices "That's true.") It was not sufficient for a woman. At any rate it was not sufficient for somebody he knew.

(Renewed laughter.) He came down there not to set them striking—that was not his object. Some of them struck the other day. They knew what he said to them—"Return to your work." If the farmers reduced their wages to 6s. a week, he would still counsel them to continue work, because in the mean time they could agitate. Would they be surprised to hear that poor Todd Mitchell, who was literally starved out of the place 25 or 26 years ago, was now independent of the Montacute farmers? (Cheers.) He was opposed to strikes, for he thought they showed a want of common sense. Let them reason the subject with the farmers, who must see the sense of the arguments used. They did not get beef steaks every day, nor grizzled mutton chops. They had the grizzle—the mutton chops other people had. (Laughter, and a voice, "We don't get bacon fat.") Many present knew that he once earned his living at the plough's tail. (A voice—"Yes, and shirt hanging out." Laughter.) You do not know the brogue of Montacute yet. You ought to have said, "Your butter clout hanging out." (Renewed Laughter.) Mr. Mitchell then detailed the history of his life previous to leaving Montacute.

He remembered when the standing wages were 7s. a week, and when an attempt was made to reduce them to 6s. The occupier of Abbey Farm wished to make that reduction. But the labourers would not have it, and the 7s. were continued. Since this agitation in the north of England he had heard that 14s., 15s., 18s., and even 20s. a week were paid, and he felt for his poor brethren in Montacute. He heartily thanked the proprietor of the

Pulman's Weekly News for the opportunity presented to him of helping the labourers of Montacute. He saw a letter in that paper showing the balance sheet of a labourer, and he thought that he could make something of it. The letter was headed "The Devonshire Labourer," and it referred to a labourer living not a hundred miles from Axminster. He added the words "Somerset, and not a 100 miles from Yeovil." He then had the letter printed on a poster, and these "Brompton sensationals," as they were termed, were sent to all parts of the country. It was stated that labourers had privileges, and were enabled to keep pigs. He would give £1 to every labourer who could show him a pig which was fed in his own stye. [Mr. Mitchell asked those who had pigs to hold up their hands in order that he might fiulfil his promise—but not one hand was held up.] Mr. Mitchell observed that not a labourer had a pig, for "thee'st never had the money to get one." (Laughter,) He had travelled upon the continent, and had made enquiries as to the wages to the agricultural labourers—particularly in France, Holland and Belgium The wages ranged from 10s. to 14s. a week, with a house to live in rent free. Labourers were divided into three classes—carters and shepherds receiving 15s. and 16s. a week. England was the richest country in the world, and yet the labourers had only lately been receiving 9s. and 10s. a week. And, had it not been for the "Brompton sensationals," he did not believe that the farmers would even then have increased their wages. He urged the men to join the union for their own benefit. His brother worked for a Montacute farmer for 7s. a week. He (the speaker) took him to London and doubled his wages. The farmer offered, if his (the speaker's) brother would return, to increase his wages to 8s. a week. He had not returned.

Mr. Mitchell then called upon—

John Hann, *alias* Jack Tacker, a very old man, who in answer to a question, said that he remembered when his master tried to reduce his wages to 6s. a week. But he would not accept of it. He was the "forehook" (first man) for more than 20 years. In harvest time, when he worked from 6 o'clock in the morning until nine at night, he could not make more than 10s. or 12s. a week. He could not now do a day's work. He received 1/6 a week and a loaf of bread from the parish, and if he could get a little work to do he did it.

Mr. Mitchell—And do you pay house rent?

Tacker—I have not paid anything since Christmas. I cannot afford it.

Wm. Chant, an elderly labourer, was called upon the platform and examined by Mr. Mitchell. He said that when he was married he received 10s. a week. But he worked at Montacute House, and there were no perquisites. Farm labourers were paid 9s. a week. He had eight children, and paid 1s. 6d. a week rent. Q.—How much butcher's meat did you have. A.—I did not eat threepenny-worth of beef in a twelvemonth.

Amelia Bull, a respectable looking woman, was called upon the platform and said that she had had 15 children. Q.—How much did your husband get a week? A.—7s. when we were first married. Q.—I suppose his wages were increased to 8s.? A.—Yes. Q.—His wages have been lately increased to 9s. A.—He has got 1s. extra. Q.—I suppose you have plenty of butcher's meat? A.—None whatever. Q.—Do you pay house rent? A.—1s. 6d. a week.

Mr. Mitchell said that he thought he had produced sufficient evidence to convince everyone that something ought to be done for the labourers. He hoped that they would become members of the union, and if they had not sufficient money to pay the deposit he would lend them some. (Cheers.)

Jacob Bull, then moved the following resolution, which was read by the chairman, the proposer not being able to read:—"Resolved that this meeting deeply sympathises with the long depressed condition of the agricultural labourers of Somerset and approves of the establishment of a branch of the National Agricultural Labourers' Union at Montacute, for the purpose of improving the condition of the labourer. And the labourers present pledge themselves to become members of the union and to use every effort to induce other labourers to do likewise." (Cheers.)

George Hunt seconded the resolution. He worked from six o'clock in the evening until twelve at night extra without complaint. At last he asked for some remuneration for the extra work, when his master replied that he ought to have spoken to him before, and refused his application. (Cries of "Shame.")

The resolution was then put to the meeting and carried unanimously amid much cheering. A large number of labourers afterwards entered their names as members of the union.

CHAPTER XXI.

THE FIRST ANNUAL WHITSUNTIDE MEETING OF FARM LABOURERS' ON HAM HILL, 1873.

From Pulman's Weekly News, Crewkerne.

THE long talked of "mass meeting" was held yesterday (Tuesday) afternoon at Ham Hill, and the novelty of the meeting, the beautiful weather, and the magnificent scenery, drew together an immense number of people—(about 20,000).

The occasion was the anniversary of the meeting held at Montacute last year, introducing "the National Labourers' Union into this part of England.

The Dorset union men had assembled at the South Western Railway Station, Yeovil, at one o'clock, and formed in procession. Most of the men wore cards in their hats. upon which the following was printed:—" The

Franchise for the agricultural labourers, 15s. a week all the year round, and no surrender." The procession consisted of several brakes and waggons, and about 200 men walked. Flags and banners were carried, the tops of the flag-poles being ornamented with sting-nettles. The Sherborne and the Street brass bands accompanied them. The streets of Yeovil were crowded. The procession passed through Preston and Odcombe, where arches of evergreens and flowers were erected, to Montacute, thence to Stoke, and on to the Hill.

The Glastonbury and Langport men assembled at Martock Railway Station, and, carrying banners, marched, headed by the Curry Rivel band, through Bower Hinton to Stoke.

The Montacute fife and drum band led the Montacute unionists, and the West Chinnock fife and drum band brought up the Chinnock and Chiselborough men.

The weather was charming, and the magnificent landscape, comprising almost the entire county of Somerset and a portion of Wiltshire, was much enjoyed.

At four oclock the processions came up by the hill, and, as they broke off by various routes to the Frying Pan, the scene was very animating. The company included a very large proportions of females whose varied dresses added greatly to the picturesqueness of the scene.

Ample preparations had been made for the visitors. Tents were erected, refreshments were in bountiful supply, gingerbread stalls were scattered about, and Aunt

Sally and other sports were provided. As the afternoon wore on, dancing and kiss-in-the-ring were thoroughly enjoyed, and nothing like " slavery " was to be seen in any direction.

At about half-past four o'clock Mr. George Mitchell, of London, a native of Montacute, the originator of the meeting, and, it is understood, the defrayer of the expenses, arrived in the Frying Pan, and the platform was formed by a break.

The Frying Pan, which centuries ago, when the Romans had succeeded in conquering Britain, was the scene of audiences of so different a character, was filled with an attentive assembly of men, women and children, and including several clergymen and other gentlemen.

On the motion of Mr. George Mitchell, Henry Atherton, Esq., an ex-Indian Judge, was voted to the chair.

Mr. Atherton was received with cheers. He had come a long distance to attend that meeting but had no idea that he should be called upon to take the chair. He could not, however, refuse to do so, for no one took a warmer interest in the movement than he did. (Cheers.) He would give them a little of his own experience as that would enable them to understand why he had such warm feelings with regard to the movement, and why he held so strongly that that movement was likely to improve the position, not only of the agricultural labourer, but also of the farmer and landlord. They had from the hill a view of the most glorious country on the face of the earth, a country which had hitherto been blessed by God's bounty, but cursed by man's folly and selfishness. But a new time was coming, when the labourer would get the due reward for his exertions, when the farmer would be paid for the trouble he took in cultivating the land, and when the landlord would be far more secure than he was under the present system. They might be assured that the feudal system was breaking up—that system which had hitherto been a curse to the country, a disgrace to religion, and altogether inconsistent with real Christianity. (Cheers.) Because it encouraged feelings of pride with which Christianity could not exist. (Cheers.) He would tell them why he took such an interest in the movement. Forty years ago he went out to the East Indies, and there during a long service he had the very best possible opportunity of noting the arrangements made for the cultivation of the land. People there were not mere hired labourers, but nearly all had an interest in the soil Under that system he had seen whole tracks of jungle and waste lands brought into cultivation. And the effect was, that during the Indian mutiny peace and quietness were maintained and the government was kept secure. (Cheers.) They must have that sort of thing in this country, and then England would be safe. They might be assured that they could not go on as they had been going with the land half cultivated and with wealth concentrated in the hands of a few. Times were changing, and the poor were no longer the ignorant serfs they had hitherto been, Education was advancing, and the press was enlightening the masses of the people. Of one thing they might be certain, that if they wanted to keep the people contented, they must fill their bellies as well as their minds. They remembered what they said of the slaves, "If they are well fed they will keep quiet." (Laughter and cheers.) They could not educate them and treat them with injustice. Experience showed that the law, to be cheerfully obeyed, must be based on justice. If they considered the present system, they would find that many of our laws were not such as they would be when the labourers had the franchise, and when the poor had a hand in making them. (Cheers.) Hitherto the laws had been made chiefly for the rich, and the consequences had been predudicial to the poor.

One word to the clergy, who were as much to blame as the landlords, for the present state of things. During the last two or three centuries, the clergy as a class, of course there were many noble exceptions, had disregarded the cause of the poor. What had been the effect? They had lost the poor. (Cheers.) Could they believe that if the clergy had stood between the rich and the poor, and whilst denouncing the sins of the poor, had warned the rich of their duties, and if justice had been administered as it should have been, they would have lost the poor as they now had. (No, no.) He hoped that a new era was advancing when the clergy and the rich would recollect their duties.

Mr. George Mitchell, of London, was received with cheers. He proposed the following resolution:—

"That this meeting deeply sympathizes with the depressed condition of the agricultural labourers of England, believing it to be a standing disgrace in the present stage of civilization and injurious to the best interests of the country, and is of opinion that measures should be adopted without delay for their social improvement and their mental elevation, and to this end we pledge ourselves to become members of the National Agricultural Labourers' Union." (Cheers.) Did they understand that? (Yes.) Did they all belong to the union? (No.) Then they ought to belong to it. It was of no use trying to help them unless they put their shoulders to the wheel. (Cheers.) He had received the following letters:—

Wood Street, Cheapside, London, E.C.
June 11, 1873.

Dear Sir,

I am sorry to say that it is out of my power to attend the Ham Hill meeting. It will give me pleasure to find that the agricultural labourers are not behind in the general advancement in social condition which has been realised so generally throughout the country of late years. They had an undoubted right to combine, not for the injury of others, but for the protection of their own welfare and the many interests they have in common. I heartily wish them continued and increased success. It can only be secured by their eschewing subjects which are foreign, and confining their action to their one immediate object of their society. I am, dear Sir, yours faithfully,

S. MORLEY.

Mr. George Mitchell.

Clapham, London.

Dear Sir,

On all occasions I defend the cause of those labourers who are oppressed in their wages, and I am only doing my duty in taking such a course. I am not, however, able to attend meetings upon the subject. There are plenty of gentlemen who are quite able to attend to this social question, and there is no need that I should turn aside from my own work. I have a ministry committed to me, and to that one thing I bend all my strength. I do not feel that I am called upon to leave my preaching of the Gospel for any work, however excellent. If I had not got a ministry to attend to I should count it a glory to fight the social battles of the agricultural labourers, and you do well to give your strength to such work. I shall always have a good word for any class that is down-trodden, for the gospel is no respecter of persons and is ever the friend of man. Yours, &c.,

C. H. SPURGEON.

House of Commons, May 27, 1873.

Dear Mr. Mitchell,

You have honoured me with an invitation to preside at a very large gathering of delegates and members of agricultural labour unions in the West of England. Speaking only for myself, and not wishing to criticise the course taken by any of my colleagues, I do not think it convenient for a member of Parliament, as such, to take part in a movement, which, however interesting it may be to all who have a genuine regard for the welfare of the least fortunate portion of all our fellow countrymen, is one based not on political grounds, but on the commercial relations between employers and employed. The business of public men in the matter is to see fair play, to repeal all that is oppressive or partial in the Masters' and Servants' Acts and the Criminal Law Amendment Act, and to give such publicity as parliamentary discussion affords to those cases, unfortunately only too frequent, in which magistrates attempt unduly to press the provisions of those acts, or to stifle the rights of public meeting in the rural districts by a very questionable application of a statute which was passed for quite another purpose.

But it is idle to expect that our agricultural labourers will get an effective hearing for their wishes and grievances as long as they are deprived of the Parliamentary Franchise. Till they are in possession of the vote they will continue to learn the bitter lesson that legislation, as in every other walk of life, out of sight is out of mind. At present they alone, of all the classes in the nation, are unable to command the attention, and are reduced to appeal to the charity of the House of Commons. It would be easy to quote passages from the works of all the great men who have in recent times written on constitutional questions to prove that, in the conflict of a Legislative Assembly, unrepresented interests infallibly go to the wall. And so it must be as long as human nature is the same inside as outside Parliament.

I am for these reasons very glad to hear from you that one of the resolutions to be proposed at the meeting is to be an expression of opinion in favour of the extension of

Household Suffrage to the counties, and I trust that this resolution will be worthily supported and carried by a decisive majority. No improvement to their condition which our labourers may obtain can be permanently kept by them as long as they alone continue to be outcasts from the pale of citizenship and subjected to a disability which has its parallel in no civilized nation, for nowhere else at the present day is the inhabitant of the country treated politically as an inferior to the inhabitant of the towns. It is painful to reflect that Britain, the mother of free institutions, still refuses to the hard-working quiet-living population of our rural districts those civic rights which the American negro has enjoyed for seven years past. As long as the people of our villages fail in getting these rights, they have secured nothing, If they acquire them, they will have gained everything,—for they will have the same chance of justice and consideration as other classes of the community, and I know enough of them to be certain that justice, and nothing beyond it, is the object of their sacrifices, their efforts, and their aspirations. I remain, dear Sir, yours truly,

GEORGE OTTO TREVELYAN.

Mr. Mitchell stated that the other day people said that Mr. Spurgeon was in league with Bradlaugh and Odger trying to upset the church. (Voice—The sooner the better.) But Mr. Spurgeon said that he had the gospel to attend to, and that was as much as he could do. Mr. Mitchell next spoke of his early association with Montacute, and pointed out the spot where he ploughed out thirteen dozen of swords. If they had paid him well he might have been there that day. But God had prospered him and he had come to help his friends in Somerset. He had come there not to tell them to fight, but to tell them their rights,—that the law, with which they had nothing to do in making, empowered them to combine. The farmers had combined, and so had the landlords. But would they be surprised if he told them that if the labourers combined they would be ten times stronger than both put together? The farmers of Somerset were trying to keep the white slaves of Somerset down. But they should not do so any longer. (Bravo.)

He wanted the men to be true to each other. They saw the mottoes upon the cards. 15s. a week was not too much for a man to keep a wife and family, and they would have "no surrender." (Cheers.) They must have 15s. a week, they should have it, and would have it. (Loud cheers, and "bravo.") They were not going to be disloyal. If they had a second suit of clothes in which to attend church or chapel, a bit of bacon in the chimney corner, a grave of "taties" in the garden, a pig in the stye, a sack or two of flour, and a place a little better than a pig has to live in, Mr. King William or Mr. Emperor Napoleon—(laughter)—or Mr. Anybody else had better not attempt to put a foot on our shores. If they had a pig in their stye they would fight for that, and if that blessed woman—the Queen—who has never been guilty of an unbecoming act, should say to them, "Drive my enemies away," they would go to a man. But if the country starved them they might just as well be in the hands of the Prussians or the French as in those of the Government. But God never ordained men to be slaves. ("No, no.") He said unhesitatingly that the labourers of England, and especially the labourers of Somerset, were worse off than the slaves of any foreign nation. The slaves in foreign countries had plenty of grub, and that was more than they (the labourers) had. (Laughter.) Mr. Mitchell then concluded by reading a piece of poetry recommending the claims of the union. (Loud cheers.)

Mr. Joseph Arch, upon rising, was loudly cheered. He said we are met here to-day upon one of the most important questions which at this time is agitating the country—a question which we must all look at whether we are landlords, farmers, labourers, or mechanics. I believe that the good of one class is the good of another, and if the agricultural labourers can be bettered in their position, can assume that position in society to which they have a just right, no class would suffer but all classes would be benefited thereby. (Cheers.) I look upon this not merely as a labourers' but as a national question—because the agricultural labourers are the feeders of the nation. (Cheers.) I challenge anyone to dispute that statement. If this class of men who feed the country are to be in a continual state of starvation and poverty, if their national interests are to be for ever tarnished, how long will you keep England in peace? How long will you settle down society into that happy condition which John Bright, in his noble speeches, so often referred to? If there be a man in England who would like to see the country prosperous, happy, and contented, it is Joseph Arch. (Cheers.)

But while I see thousands of a class to which I have the honour to belong, placed in houses where a farmer would not put his cattle, with starvation wages from week to week, and with no better prospect when their work is done than the wards of a union workhouse, then I say there is no man who would raise his voice louder, who would use his energies with more moral and physical force, than Joseph Arch, to bring those men to their true position.

Mr. Taylor, the general secretary of the National Agricultural Labourers' Union, moved that a petition be presented to the House of Commons in favour of the bill for the reduction of the county franchise. Mr. Taylor detailed the programme of the union, its objects and strength, and stated that it numbered 70,000 members. He showed that its committee consisted of members of Parliament, clergymen, and others, and that strikes would not be resorted to unless through sheer necessity. He alluded to the Sheffield trade union outrages, and said that for every one which could be pointed out he could give forty instances of acts committed by squires, farmers, and clergymen equally as bad as those of Broadhead.

Mr. John Mitchell, J.P., of Lyme Regis, was received with loud cheers. He seconded the resolution with a great deal of pleasure. He came there to take part in the proceedings from a sense of humanity and good feeling towards the industrial classes. He had all to lose and nothing to gain by the movement. (Cheers.) He had during the past twelve years been located in the neighbouring county of Dorset, and had had an opportunity of seeing and judging as to the condition of the agricultural labourer. He had found the labourers to be most industrious, hard-working, and honest men. That was more than he could say of some of his neighbours. For that very reason he had taken their interest at heart, and had endeavoured to improve their condition. He hoped that the enfranchisement of the labourers would soon become a fact, believing that the labourers would exercise it with as much discretion as the parties who now held it. He should be glad to see the labourer represented in Parliament. Until they had an opportunity of sending a representative to Parliament he did not think they might expect to have their condition bettered.

Mr. George Potter was received with three times three. He said that that time last year he had the honour of taking the chair down in the borough of Montacute, and of addressing many of them who had never before heard anything of the movement the anniversary of which they were then celebrating. A great many persons said that it would begin in the Borough, die in the Borough, and be buried in the Borough. (No, no, and laughter.) It was born in the borough, and it would never die so long as England lived. He then told the labourers that the country was in a prosperous condition, and that the farmers could afford to give higher wages. The country now was more prosperous than it was last year. The farmers had raised their wages a little, but before that time next year, their wages would be again increased. He told them last year that they would have many enemies and that their meetings would be pooh-poohed and ridiculed. They had had many enemies, and the movement had been ridiculed. The more enemies they had had and the more they ridiculed the movement the greater it had become. (Loud cheers.) It sprang up like a mushroom, it now lived like a giant oak, and underneath its branches men, women and children, rejoiced together. (Loud cheers.) He was there to congratulate the men of Somerset. They had done wonders. Last year they did not know that they had a soul of their own. But they now knew that they were men, and that they could assert their independence. He was there to say, "Go on in your movement, and the country will ultimately recognise it as one of the greatest blessings the English farm labourers ever had."

He asked the women to make their husbands join the union, and the young ladies to insist upon the young men becoming members previous to marriage. Instead of having a meeting from twenty miles round, the meeting that time next year would take in an area of 50 miles round, and everybody would want to come to Ham Hill. Although the Frying Pan was very big it would not be large enough to fry them all. (Laughter and cheers.) He looked to the future. He could look back 15 years when he joined a union as a carpenter and joiner, and to the grand results achieved by a union in the artizan trades. He looked beyond the present, and to the time when England would be proud of the tillers of her soil and not ashamed of the "degraded lot." The labourers ought to look forward to the time when their children would be men and women, who would be as superior to them in comfort, in intelligence, and in pecuniary position, as the sun was to the stars. They were building up a future for their children, who would bless them for having joined the union. Could anything else have effected the enormous increase in their position in so short a time as the union? (No, no, and cheers.)

Cheers were then given for the Union, for Messrs. George Mitchell and Arch, and for the Chairman, and the proceedings terminated.

Very large parties then spent the remainder of the evening in dancing to the music of the bands.

Upon the second platform Mr. Ball, who describes himself as a "Lincolnshire labourer," took the chair. He said that it was a marvel to find that the farm labourers had come out in the way they had. But their cause was righteous, and they were not ashamed to meet together and tell their grievances to the world. The Hill had never witnessed such a sight before as it had that day, nor would that meeting have been held but for the down-trodden state in which the farm labourers were. That day would leave its mark in the history of the nation which would never be erased until the last man died.

Mr. Smith, from Gloucester, said that he was very pleased to have the opportunity of meeting them. Although he lived in Glo'stershire he was bred and born in Somerset, and had a great deal of sympathy with the labourers' claims, and, as soon as he heard of the meeting being about to be held, he determined to come among them and try to help them out of the mire.

Mr. Yates, of Gloucester, then moved the following

resolution :—" That it is the opinion of this meeting that the county franchise should be assimilated with the borough franchise, and that there should be a thorough re-distribution of seats."

Mr. Mayor, district secretary of Dorset, seconded the resolution, and addressed the meeting at considerable length.

Mr. Gould, of Yeovil, and Mr. Wedmore, a delegate, also delivered speeches.

CHAPTER XXII.

Prejudice, Persecution and Prosecution.

THE Montacute branch of the labourers' union soon enrolled over 500 members, and the movement spread all over the county. Some of the greatest cruelties were practised by parsons, magistrates, and farmers, on men who joined the union. One poor shepherd who had thus provoked the wrath of his master was sent to prison for 6 months with hard labour. He was a man of irreproachable character, and had been a highly respectable member of the Wesleyan body for 20 years. I have no hesitation in saying that he had no more idea of doing a dishonest act than had the magistrate who convicted him. The case was as follows :—

"William Osmond, of Charlton Horethorne, Somerset, is about 56 years of age, and for the last 20 years has worked on a farm at Milborne Wick, Milborne Port, and for the same employer. Fifteen years of his time, he had been employed as Shepherd. His wages for the most part have been 8s., 9s. and 10s. a week, Sunday included, and for the whole of the 15 years he has had besides his wages, a cottage value 1s. per week, 1 ton of coal per annum, potato ground value 20s. per annum, 6d., for every twin lamb at the end of the season, and the sale of the surplus lambs, which is the custom of the country, and this has always been left to his discretion.

This perquisite has been granted as a reward for the great care and attention required at the lambing season. Last year, Osmond was known to have passed 5 to 6 weeks without going home to his bed.

The flock (being horn sheep and well kept, watched and cared for) have been very prolific, and on some previous seasons Osmond has sold many more lambs than those sold last season, as from some cause peculiar to the season, many lambs were lost, but, notwithstanding this, at the close of the season Osmond had not a single ewe without a lamb, besides which he had 30 couples. About this time Osmond joined the Labourers' Union and advised his fellow workmen to join also. This annoyed his master who had previously cautioned him, and about three months after the sale of the lambs (of which the master knew, as is the custom) one night early in March, 1873, just as Osmond was going to bed, two policemen entered his cottage, charged him wlth stealing a large number of lambs, and at once led him 5 miles to the lock-up, where he remained two days and two nights.

When the case was heard by the Magistrates, who showed no disposition to inquire into the custom and who were possibly more anxious to please the farmers than to do justice, Osmond was committed for trial at the Taunton Sessions. Bail, to their surprise, was soon found. At the Sessions, Osmond was defended, but the jurymen were divided, ten being in favour of an acquittal and two (farmers) against; they were locked up, and the result was a verdict of 'Guilty' with a recommendation to mercy, and a sentence to 6 months hard labour.

A similar case was tried the next day, in the same court and by the same jury, and the man (Edward Forward, not belonging to the N.A.L.U.) was acquitted, although he had sold nine more lambs out of a smaller flock.

We add that no lambs had been sold for nearly three months previous to the charge being made."

On the liberation of this man a grand demonstration took place at Taunton and a purse of sovereigns (£20) was presented to him as a testimonial to his innocence and fidelity to the Union, to which cause he had become a martyr. The superiority of prison diet over that of a shepherd was noted by all who knew this persecuted man. In six months he had gained twenty-three pounds of flesh and appeared much more healthy and robust than when he entered the gaol, so that his enemies, though they had disgraced him in the eyes of unthinking people, had done him rather a service by respiting him for awhile from the starving slavery of farm labour and promoting him to indoor employment with better food.

The farmer who prosecuted, or rather persecuted this man, knew that he was doing wrong, but his hatred of the union blinded him to all sense of right, and he snapped a conviction against this worthy man who had faithfully served him for so many years. The prosecutor soon after died, it is said of sheer remorse, for he scarcely ever held up his head after Osmond's imprisonment. Many shallow grandees of the provinces thought that these harsh measures would stamp out the union, and they were determined that the snake should not only be scotched, but killed altogether.

Men, women and children, were turned out of house and home, their poor little goods and chattels being thrown out on the roadside, merely to gratify the spite of landlords and farmers against the movement, which the occupant had dared to join. If any doubt this statement, let them apply to Mr. Mayor, of Blandford, for photographs of the union evictions in Dorsetshire, and they will see "doust" beds, deal tables, ricketty chairs and old boxes in most admired disorder, with the poor unionist's wives and babies, sitting disconsolately among their scattered furniture.

As for myself, I was called everything but a gentlemen that Billingsgate could invent. I was numbered with the "agitators who go about setting class against class" who the Bishop of Gloucester and other clergymen advised should be thrown into horseponds, merely because we were doing a part of their duties, I suppose, for whether

Mr. Spurgeon is or is not right as to his sense of the duties devolving upon him, surely the rural clergy of a church attached to the state ought to take some steps to prevent the starvation of their parishioners, at least they should raise their voices against it.

Every kind of attempt, legal and illegal, has been made to injure me and the cause I espouse, but we prosper yet, and I would remind those gentlemen who refuse me their friendship and support on account of my opinions and public acts, that they may be fighting against a power to which their opposition is futile, and that a time may come when they will regret that they were on the wrong side.

Signed: G. MITCHELL,
"One from the Plough."

CHAPTER XXIII.

Where are we now?

LET us briefly sketch out the farm labourer's grievances as they exist at the present time, for many well disposed readers will say—" Ah, those bad times were long ago," and they will congratulate themselves on living, not only in the nineteenth century but in the last quarter of that century, when such scandals as are herein exposed have no existence. Again we would say "Lay not this flattering unction to your souls"— the state of the agricultural labourer this very day is not greatly improved, notwithstanding all that has been done for him.

True, wages have been raised some two or three shillings per week through the efforts of the union, but that is a mere instalment of justice due, and is scarcely sufficient to be felt at all in the matter of food, prices having had an upward tendency all the while.

What are the average wages of the poor farm labourers of the West at this present time? What are the requirements of a working man's family? These are the two great practical questions to be answered in order to demonstrate our case beyond all cavil or sophistry.

In the Autumn of 1874, Mr. Fawcett, M.P., wrote to the *Times* to complain that the wages of the Wiltshire labourers which had been 12/- during the Summer had been reduced to 11/- on account of the bountiful harvest! The member for Hackney also deprecated a system of keeping men down to mere *subsistence wages*. We quite agree with Professor Fawcett that such a system is degrading in the extreme, but we fail to see anything like a subsistence in 11/- or 12/- per week, and be it remembered that TEN SHILLINGS may be regarded as the average wage of the West of England Agricultural Labourer, since six, seven and eight were the figures before the agitation, and, as yet, the improvement has been three shillings at the most.

The following letter published in "*The Times*," of October 16, 1874, will explain our position.—

Before discussing the question if it is right that

farm labourers should be kept down to the level of subsistence wages, will you permit me to ask if they ever get subsistence wages?

It is now quite clear what the wages in South Wilts are—Eleven shillings! and yet your correspondent "A South Wilts Farmer" in your issue of October 2, says "Professor Fawcett is certainly not justified in saying that our labourers 'are in a condition of such miserable dependence and poverty that the wages they receive are simply subsistence wages, or, in other words, are determined by considering what is the *minimum* upon which a labourer and his family can exist.'"

To show that Professor Fawcett was above the mark, and did not represent the state of the labourer in its worst colours, I have drawn up a list of necessaries for a man, his wife, and his family of four children (a low average, unfortunately, for the poor farm labourers); and I will ask any humane person if it is an extravagant estimate of ordinary necessaries of the humblest kind, and if it is more than a mere subsistence after all?

Let us see how much per week a subsistence amounts to:—

	£	s.	d.
House rent - - - - - - -	0	1	6
One dozen of bread, at 7d., unweighed in the country) - - - - - -	0	7	0
Meat at 8d. per lb., allowing ½lb. a day for a whole family - - - - -	0	2	4
1½lb. of cheese, at 8d. - - - - -	0	1	0

	£	s.	d.
1½lb. of sugar, at 4d.	0	0	6
¼lb. of tea, at 2/4	0	0	7
1½lb. of butter, at 1/2	0	1	9
Candles or oil	0	0	6
Fuel (1cwt. coal)	0	1	6
Clothing	0	1	0
Boots and shoes one pair each per annum	0	1	0
Washing materials (soap, starch, &c.)	0	0	4
Needlework repairs, &c.	0	0	2
Salt and pepper	0	0	1
Schooling	0	0	4
Benefit club	0	0	4
Treacle	0	0	3
Tools	0	0	2
Furniture, bedding and sundries	0	0	8
Total	1	1	0

Now, this shows that the man is earning only about half subsistence wages, and is inta worse condition upon 11/- per week than the Professor describes! and as to making those wages higher by piecework in harvest, I assert and maintain, and can prove, that what he gains by overstrained exertions in harvest time, often ruinous to his constitution, he more than loses by loss of time in wet and frosty weather (averaging six weeks, according to the Blue book of Her Majesty's Commissioner, the Hon. Mr. Stanhope); and I happen to know that this 11/- per week exists only upon paper, being paid partly in goods, cottage or allotment at the farmer's own price, falsely called perquisites.

I am, Sir, Yours faithfully,
G. MITCHELL,
"One from the Plough."

In the course of the lengthy and clever leader upon this letter with which we were honoured by the Jupiter of the press, the writer says:—

"Mr. G. Mitchell, 'One from the Plough,' comes forward, at the invitation of Professor Fawcett, to state on behalf of the Labourer what is the *minimum* upon which he and his family can exist. Accordingly we are presented with a highly authoritative estimate, which ought to be a most important contribution not merely to the agricultural controversy, but even to a just notion of all human affairs. If it is necessary to know the range and the limits of the human knowledge and human power, so it is also to know at what cost an ordinary degree of vital energy can be maintained. Mr. Mitchell's calculation for this purpose is, however, so widely at variance with that which prevails, not only in Wiltshire, but we might say all over the Old World, that we are forcibly and painfully reminded of innumerable occasions when a similar problem has led to similar divergencies of estimate. What can a man live upon? What can a man marry upon? What is absolutely necessary for dress, for education, and the requirements of society? What must a man have at college? What is the lowest decent clerical stipend? What is the very least we should give to a bishop, a Minister, an Ambassador, or a Prince of the Blood?

in the scale. The more personal and even homely the wants, the more we disagree."

But no essayist in the world, be he of forty Macaulay power, can annihilate facts, or reconcile the difficulties of the peasant who requires a guinea's worth of food and other necessaries to make life bearable for seven days, and who only obtains half a guinea for his six days—(often 7 days) labour.

Upon the same letter the *Evening Standard* said—

"We will not quarrel with the table further than to point out that the sum expended in indifferent butter might be devoted to something more nourishing. But having drawn up this table of "necessaries," and having described it as a table of mere " subsistence expenditure," allowing nothing whatever for beer or medicine, or any luxuries, Mr. Mitchell goes on to say concerning his hypothetical man :—

" Now, this shows that the man is earning only about half subsistence wages ; and, as to making those wages higher by piecework in harvest, I assert and maintain, and can prove, that what he gains by overstrained exertions in harvest, often ruinous to his constitution, he more than loses by loss of time in wet and frosty weather (averaging six weeks, according to the Blue Book of Her Majesty's Commissioner, the Hon. Mr. Stanhope) and I happen to know that this 11s. per week exists only upon paper, being paid partly in goods, cottage, or allotment at the farmer's own price, falsely called perquisites." It must be admitted that Mr. Mitchell has something more than proved his case. He has shown clearly that in order to maintain life, the average Wiltshire labourer has to spend 21/- a week. He has also shown that the earnings are less than half that sum. The obvious conclusion is that the Wiltshire labourer does not "subsist." And if he does not "subsist" how can he exist? People cannot but see that somewhere or other there must be a flaw in the reasoning which would make out that men on whose behalf this appeal is made, all died of starvation years ago."

Now, the *Evening Standard* is an excellent newspaper, and has, doubtless, done great work for its party. The liberal government ought never to have allowed the *Evening Star* to die out, as they were just doubling the influence of the *Evening Standard*, which has played the part of Lady Sneerwell so admirably, as to powerfully assist in sneering Messrs. Gladstone & Co. out of office. If this vesper organ has succeeded in doing so much to upset a people's government, it is not strange that it was capable of ridiculing our plain statement of fact in *The Times*.

What does the argument of the *Evening Standard* amount to? Why just this—that because we proved only a half subsistence and a state of semi-starvation, we proved that the farm labourers were paid "nothing a week and find themselves," and that they have all died of starvation! This is just as though the *Standard* should receive a telegram to the effect that a number of shipwrecked sailors had endured terrible privations through want of water, and should publish it to the world that they had all died of thirst! The sailors might have been in great straits for want of water, such as sucking the rain out of their clothes, or drinking sea-water, and they might be reduced to skeletons, as very thin persons are often termed in common parlance, without positively dying, nor yet could their allowance of water be called a subsistence supply. The farm labourers are just in this plight as regards food—they do exist, though they have no proper subsistence.

CHAPTER XXIV.

The Cause and the Cure.

AND now what remains to be said? Much more could be written upon this wretchedness and degradation existing in our rural districts. Much could be written upon this topic which would be totally unfit for print. We however, forbear for the present to make further disclosures as to the condition of the Poor Farm Labourers of the West. If any should doubt the truth of our statements, let them search into the matter for themselves. They will speedily find in our villages much that words could not and should not express—hideous vices, appalling immorality in life and conversation—all the result of poverty and ignorance.

At whose door does this evil lie? First and foremost,

the landlords of this country are to blame. Their utter selfishness, which we cannot but regard as low and mean, has caused them to appropriate to themselves generation after generation, by all sorts of artful and cunning tricks, every yard of the earth's surface.

Next, the parsons are verily guilty in this matter. They have shown very little energy in attempting to improve the state of their parishioners—they have allowed them to remain in ignorance. The education they *have* imparted has been of a depressing rather than an elevating character. That catechism which enjoins lowly reverence to their " betters " to anybody, in fact, who chooses to set themselves in authority over them, has made too many of them slavish and hypocritical. These gentlemen have mostly taken to preaching and parish work, just as they would have taken to the army or the law, merely because it gained them income and position, and as they are generally poor relations of the lord or the squire, they have not dared to remonstrate with their rich friends either in public or private.

The farmers are to blame, though they have been kept in a state of such insecurity and dependence on the landlords, that they have been afraid to part with a shilling more than absolutely necessary to keep the bodies and souls of their people together. They are to blame because they have not unanimously striven to emancipate themselves from the thrall of an annual tenure through which they have been unable to cultivate the land to its utmost value. How would a merchant develop his business if some other man had the opportunity of ousting him next year? The farmer is in the position of a tradesman with a bill of sale over his head, and thus his credit is injured, so that he cannot extend his operations beyond a very limited sphere.

Lord Derby, in a speech at Liverpool, declared that the land of England, which was in cultivation, might easily produce double the crops now obtained. No doubt, this is (as is usual with Lord Derby) a moderate estimate of the capabilities of our soil, and it is needless to add that these capabilities can never be developed under the present system of uncertain tenure.

But the farmers are to blame for the crafty way in which they have kept down the poor labourers, not only by miserably inadequate wages, but by keeping back portions of the paltry silver for various things supposed to be supplied at a loss, but really, at an enormous profit—light grist corn unfit for the market at 6s. per bushel, yielding so badly that the women may say "Oh, my dear flour!" when they get it. Then that very poor cider, or sad small beer, representing one fourth of the income of a family!

As to the cottages—what of them? The farmers rent them of the landlords at a "pepper-corn" and let them to the men at a rental of 1/6 or 2/- a week, with the promise that they continue to work for starvation wages—so that the humble tenant is kept in precisely the same fear by the farmer as is the farmer by the landlord. A reign of terror is the consequence. Fiends are ever whispering in the ears of both master and man:—"You may be turned out," and both become servile in consequence.

We could speak of common lands taken from the people by the order of county magistrates, often for their own benefit, of estates left for charitable purposes being let at nominal rents, which have been purposely left unpaid, the lands never returning to the charities to which they were given. We could point out the millions of acres of good land lying barren or wasted for ornamental purposes while the aborigines, the descendents of the original possessors, are starving upon these fine estates.—We could tell of smug policemen swearing away the liberty of young fellows for being in the same field as a few rabbits, whereby, aged parents, losing their support, have been removed to workhouses and their squatter cottages have thereby become absorbed. We could demonstrate to all who are not blinded by the profits of silver shrine making, that a system of cruel injustice exists in the West of England not to be exceeded by the practices of Turkish Pachas! But for the present we forbear to make further disclosures—In brief conclusion we have now to consider the remedies for these evils, and we merely tabulate them as follows.

1.—The franchise for the Agricultural Labourers.

2.—Education; free, secular, and compulsory.

3.—A School-board in every parish.

4.—Perfect religious equality, so that every theological tub shall stand on its own bottom.

5.—A complete repeal of the Game Laws, so that a distinction can be made between wild and domestic animals.

6.—Tenant rights for the farmers on really equitable terms, not permissive but compulsory.

7,—A fair day's wages for a fair day's work, paid in hard cash with no abatements whatever, in order that a man may *live* and not *starve* by the sweat of his brow.

8.—Decent homes for the farm labourers, held by them from the landlords and not from their masters.

9.—Allotments of land sufficient for the personal requirements of the men, at the same price per acre as the fields let to the farmers.

10.—Civility, liberty, plenty and peace to all and for all.

Printed by
H. & W. Brown. 261, Brompton Road, London, S.W.

www.ingramcontent.com/pod-product-compliance
Lightning Source LLC
LaVergne TN
LVHW061215060426
835507LV00016B/1944